Unique Travel Guides

www.uniquetravelguides.com

DISCLAIMER

Although the author and publisher have made every effort to ensure that the information in this book was correct at the time of going to press, the author and publisher do not assume and hereby disclaim any liability to any party for any loss, damage, or disruption caused by errors or omissions.

Please check with the necessary organisations before making any travel plans.

DISCLAIMER 1

INTRODUCTION 4

WHO ARE UNIQUE TRAVEL GUIDES? 4

HOW TO USE THIS GUIDE 5

PASSES AND DISCOUNTS 7

GETTING AROUND 10

ARUNDEL CASTLE AND GARDENS 12

BATH 15

BRIGHTON 22

BLUEBELL RAILWAY 29

CAMBRIDGE 33

CANTERBURY 38

CHISLEHURST CAVES 43

COLCHESTER 44

EASTBOURNE 48

GROOMBRIDGE PLACE 53

HAMPTON COURT PALACE 58

HIGHCLERE CASTLE (DOWNTON ABBEY) 60

THE MAKING OF HARRY POTTER 62

HEVER CASTLE 64

HUNDRED ACRE WOOD - HOME OF WINNIE THE POOH & FRIENDS 69

KEW GARDENS 72

LEEDS CASTLE 77

THE NEW FOREST 79

OXFORD 85

PARIS 95

ROCHESTER 101

STONEHENGE 104

SALISBURY 108

SANDRINGHAM 111

STRATFORD-UPON-AVON 115

TWICKENHAM 124

WARWICK CASTLE 126

WEMBLEY 129

WHITSTABLE 131

WIMBLEDON 134

WINCHESTER 136

WINDSOR & ETON 141

YORK 148

THANK YOU 154

INTRODUCTION

Whether you are staying in London for a week, or a whole month, you won't have enough time to visit each experience on offer. London is a city that enriches you in a unique way with each and every visit.

So, with that in mind, why would you even want to consider taking a day trip out of the city? Well, it would be a shame to not fully appreciate life outside of London. As incredible as London is, when you step outside the city, you get a real flavour of English life.

England is a compact country with excellent transport links. This makes it very feasible to see a lot more of the country than just the capital. Depending on your interests, there is a diverse and unique choice of places to see. The historic university cities of Cambridge and Oxford, or the fun of the seaside with a train ride to Brighton. Perhaps you want to indulge your literacy side and visit Shakespeare's country or immerse yourself in Hogwarts, with a studio visit to the Harry Potter experience. You can have your pick of historical castles with Windsor, Arundel, Hever, Warwick and Leeds all an option.

Not all day trips are in England either. It is very possible to catch a train from London all the way to Paris in time for breakfast.

33 Day Trips from London details a wide range of opportunities to take a day or 2 out of your London itinerary to sample a bit of the rest of England, and further afield.

So, dive in and get inspired by all the amazing places you can see on your next trip to London.

WHO ARE UNIQUE TRAVEL GUIDES?

Casares, Spain

4

Hello, my name is Kate Paulwell and I am the dreamer and traveller behind Unique Travel Guides. But, I do not work alone – I have the trusty help of my researchers, who include my husband, and our three slightly cheeky children.

Having lived in and experienced a variety of different destinations across the globe, we currently live in the county of Dorset in England. We are fortunate enough that we have had plenty of opportunities to explore and travel the world, both before we had children, and now, with them. Our trips have ranged from a year around the world, to 3 months in Europe, and everything else in between.

I actively encourage my children to get inspired about visiting other corners and cultures of our amazing globe. And if we can't always go far, we have an immense abundance of beauty right on our own doorstep.

I am a strong believer that to only experience one place, is akin to only reading one page in a book.

If you are interested in finding out about the places we go, we have recently launched a travel blog which can be found at **www.familyontour.co.uk.**

Day Trips from London began from my own years of researching and going on our own day trips from London. However, what I once envisioned to be a mini guide featuring around 10 destinations, rapidly grew to something much bigger. Of course, I couldn't include every possible day trip from London, although I would like to give it a go one day! I have however included the classics with the lesser knowns. I hope you enjoy the mix.

Thank You

I really appreciate the time you have taken to purchase and read my book. In today's digital world we can sometimes suffer from information overload. I absolutely love to hear from people – if you want to connect with me in any way, please do so via **kate@uniquetravelguides.com** – I always answer each email I receive. Let's talk travel! I will mention this one more time at the end of the book as a little reminder, but if you gain anything of use from this guide, I would be beyond grateful if you could please take a little time to offer your review on Amazon. This really does help my book become more visible among the bigger names out there, and I will of course, be eternally thankful.

Happy Travels!

Kate x

HOW TO USE THIS GUIDE

I hope each destination will provide you with enough inspiration and information to make a decision as to whether you want to do it as a day trip from London. Some places also include an 'In the Area' section where I have given some suggestions of other places you might be interested in. Perhaps they might sway you to take an overnight stay in one of the places.

How long you should/could spend in a place is a tough question to answer. I have provided loose suggestions where applicable. For some, it isn't appropriate. For example, a city such as Oxford or Bath can easily demand a whole day, depending on your interests, and you will have only scratched the surface. Perhaps you only have half a day to spare – don't let this put you off going, something is better than nothing and it will give you an insight to what a place is like. Some people like to fit as many places in as possible, whereas others prefer to see less, but spend more time at each experience. There is no right or wrong approach. Each day trip gives an overview of the highlights of a destination or attraction. It is by no means a conclusive guide – many of the places warrant their own guide to do them justice.

As I mentioned earlier on, I am not able to include every day trip from London in this one guide, but, if you think I have missed one out that should really, really be in here, then please email me at **kate@uniquetravelguides.com** and I will take a look and consider it for edition 2!

PASSES AND DISCOUNTS

Sometimes, with a little forward planning, you can save not only money, but also time, by booking in advance.

Passes

Some passes offer fantastic value for money and are worth considering if you will be visiting a few of the destinations.

London Pass

If you are staying in London and planning on seeing some of the big attractions, this pass is worth consideration, in my opinion. It also includes entry to the following places included in this book; Windsor Castle, Kew Gardens, Wembley Stadium Tour, Twickenham Rugby Museum & Stadium Tour, Wimbledon Lawn Tennis Museum & Tour Experience and Chislehurst Caves. But, before you make any purchases, make sure you compare the cost of entry using other offers, such as the travel by train 2 for 1 deals (mentioned below.) This might work out cheaper if you are taking the train to a lot of places.
www.londonpass.com

2 For 1 Offers When You Go By Train

When you travel by train you might be entitled to a 2 for 1 entry deal. You simply present your train ticket at the entry of the attraction for your discount. For an up to date full list of attractions please check the website below. The following places (mentioned in this book) were included at the time of writing; Hampton Court Palace, Kew Gardens, Strawberry Hill, Twickenham Rugby Museum & Stadium Tour, Wembley Stadium Tour, Wimbledon Lawn Tennis Museum.
www.daysoutguide.co.uk

National Trust

Annual membership is available for individuals and families, payable either by monthly direct debit or a one off payment. Membership includes entry and parking at over 300 historic houses, gardens, countryside and coastline spaces. Touring passes are also available for overseas visitors for 7 or 14 days duration. Prices start at £25 for 1, £45 for 2 and £50 for a family.

Memberships are available for USA visitors via the Royal Oak Foundation **www.royal-oak.org**. Agreements are in place with 14 similar heritage organisations in other countries, meaning NT members in the UK can benefit from free visiting agreements in those places, and vice versa.
www.nationaltrust.org.uk

English Heritage

Annual membership is available for unlimited access to over 400 historic places in England, including castles, historic gardens, world famous prehistoric sites and more. Up to 6 children can go free with one adult member (up to the age of 19.) Membership also entitles you to money off other attractions and reduced or free entry to various organised events throughout the year.

Prices are £51 for an adult, £88 for 2 adults and £41 for concessions.

Passes are also available for overseas visitors as either a 9 day or 16 day pass. Starting at £30 for a 9 day pass for 1 adults, £50 for 2 adults and £55 for a family (2 adults and 4 family members living at the same address, under the age of 19). 16 day passes cost £35 for an adult, £60 for 2 adults and £65 for a family.
www.english-heritage.org.uk

Historic Royal Palaces

Annual membership is available from £47 a year which allows you unlimited entry to the Tower of London, Hampton Court Palace and Kensington Palace.
www.hrp.org.uk

Train Friends & Family

If you are planning on getting to places by train then it might be worth buying an annual Friends & Family train pass. The £30 pass lasts for 12 months and entitles up to 4 adults when travelling with up to 4 children (aged 5-15) to get a 1/3 off adult train prices and 60% off for children's train fares.

To illustrate the savings that can be made, if we, as a family of 2 adults and 3 children were to decide we wanted to travel from London to Bath, and we decided that we wanted to go on July 16th 2015 (a random date picked 2 months in the future) it would cost us, for all 5 passengers, £54.70 return with the Friends & Family Railcard, as opposed to £101.50 return without it.

A saving of £46.80, so already the cost of our pass has been covered, and some more.

Great savings can still be made when train tickets are not booked so far in advance, I just looked up the same return train journey as above for a week away and the cost was £86.05 with the rail card and £159.25 without, a saving of £73.20. But of course, as I keep on mentioning, the further in advance you book, the higher the savings!
www.familyandfriends-railcard.co.uk

Two Together Train Pass

Similar to the friends and family pass, a 'Two Together' pass is available for £30 for 2 named people (over the age of 16) travelling together. Passengers get 1/3 off Standard, First Class Anytime, Off-Peak and Advanced Fares.
www.twotogether-railcard.co.uk

For a complete and thorough lowdown on trains in both the UK and worldwide, please check out 'The Man in Seat 61.' It is a fascinating website and a font of knowledge.
www.seat61.com

Discounts

Before you buy any tickets it is really worth doing a quick 'Google' to see if any current special offers are running. We always do this and quite often something will come up. Also, sign up at the voucher websites mentioned below to be alerted to any deals (using an email address solely for this purpose if you don't want to be bombarded with other emails!)

Also, when you are next in the supermarket, double check the cereal aisle. Quite often, especially in the lead up to summer, cereal boxes or similar will have entry deals on them.

www.groupon.co.uk
www.wowcher.co.uk
www.vouchercodes.co.uk
www.Hotukdeals.com
www.myvouchercodes.co.uk
www.local.amazon.co.uk
www.travelbird.co.uk
www.daysout.co.uk

As an example, today (22nd May 2015) there is a deal for Premium Tours on Amazon Local to buy a day trip to Stonehenge and Bath, including fast track entry into Stonehenge. The tour lasts 11 hours with hotel pick up. The cost is normally £79 for an adult, but through www.local.amazon.co.uk it is currently £39.

As with all these deals though, please do read the small print and make sure that you are able to use the voucher when you need to. Check on **www.moneysavingexpert.com** which has a frequently updated list of cheap days out and voucher codes.

Reward Cards

We quite often use our supermarket reward cards for discounted or free entry into places. We mainly use Tesco Clubcard but Nectar is also good. We have been to loads of places using our Clubcard vouchers. Some of the larger deals we've had have included; return flights to Spain for 5 people, 10 days camping on the Isle of Wight (including return ferry crossing), entry for 5 to the Eden Project, Legoland and countless dinners at Pizza Express.

The use of reward cards, whether using supermarket cards, credit cards or other schemes, is a fantastic way of saving money. To fully appreciate the extent to which you can use this to your advantage goes beyond the scope of this book. If you want to learn more, the above mentioned Money Saving Expert is a fantastic resource, as are **www.headforpoints.com** and **www.travelhacking.org**

GETTING AROUND

Depending on where you are visiting, will determine what mode of transport suits you better. The following resources will hopefully help you plan accordingly.

Train – Make Savings by Planning Ahead

There are regular and direct trains leaving London. My biggest tip, especially for the longer distance journeys, would be to book as far ahead in advance as you can. You can get some huge discounts. Advance tickets are journey specific though, so don't miss the train.

To give you an example, if you decided you wanted to visit York for the day, on the map it looks quite a distance. However, it is perfectly feasible to do the day trip by train as Virgin Trains take just under 2 hours to get there from Kings Cross. But won't it be really expensive? Yes, it can be if you book on the day or close to the day. Take a look at the following findings;

If you were to book a train ticket today (Friday 15thMay), for travel on Monday 18th May 2015, it would cost you £37.75 each way (with limited train times left available.) However, if you were to book today, for travel on Friday 7th August train tickets would cost £13 each way, with a pick of times. A saving of almost £50.
www.nationalrail.co.uk

TIP – If you have skipped past my **'Passes & Discounts'** chapter, head on back to see what further savings can be made when buying a train pass.

Coach

Coach travel can often equal the cheapest form of transport. However, do consider that it will more than likely take the longest too. If you are only going on a day trip, spending 3 hours each way on a coach really doesn't make sense. But, should you decide you want to use the coach;

Mega Bus

They offer some great value tickets, some tickets are as low as £1 so really worth checking out.
www.uk.megabus.com

National Express

National Express are a well-known coach company in the UK. As with most transport, the further in advance that you book, the better the discounts. They also have a range of offers and discount cards available. For example, if you buy a Family Coach Card for £8 (valid for 1 year) a child can travel free with a full paying adult.
www.nationalexpress.com

Car

If you are not from the UK, the following might be useful if you were not already aware;

• Drive on the left
• All drivers and passengers must wear a seatbelt
• You must not drive whilst holding a mobile phone or other device
• Car seats must be used for children under the age of 12 or 138cm in height
• Most cars use a manual transmission – if you would prefer automatic you will need to specify this when hiring your car
• Make yourself familiar with the Highway Code before driving. **www.gov.uk** (Highway Code)
• For full legal requirements please check at **www.dft.gov.uk**

• Parking in busy towns and cities can sometimes be challenging during peak times, allow extra time and plan accordingly. For help with planning your journey, AA Route Planner **(www.theaa.com)** is really useful, as is Google Maps. **www.google.co.uk/maps**

There are plenty of choices when it comes to rental car companies in London. You can compare prices with **www.travelsupermarket.com.** Do consider a few things before you hire a car. On week days (between 9am and 6pm) there is the London Congestion Charge for driving in London (currently £11.50 per day.) Please check the official website for the latest information. **www.tfl.gov.uk**

Also plan ahead for parking and factor in any car park charges you might incur.

Organised Tours

An organised tour can save a lot of time and cover much more ground than if you are juggling train times. Additionally, they often come with knowledgeable tour guides who can provide you with background information on where you are going. In no particular order of preference, here are some of the main tour companies who provide day trips from London.

Evan Evans Tours – www.evanevanstours.com
London Walks – www.walks.com
Premium Tours – www.premiumtours.co.uk
Golden Tours – www.goldentours.com
City Sightseeing – www.city-sightseeing.com
Hop on Hop off Bus – www.hop-on-hop-off-bus.com

ARUNDEL CASTLE AND GARDENS

Credit – VisitEngland/Arundel

This Grade I listed building has been in the ownership and also home to the family of the Duke of Norfolk, and their ancestors, for almost 1,000 years. Arundel Castle is an imposing and striking castle, commanding your attention as soon as you enter the town of Arundel. The castle is in amazing condition and is well presented, having been restored during the 18th and 19th centuries due to damage in the English Civil War. Arundel Castle is a popular visitor attraction and has been for some time, the keep, grounds and gatehouse has been open to the public since 1800!

As striking as the castle is, the gardens and grounds are equally as impressive, so factor in enough time to fully appreciate them.

The Castle (open March 28th – Sunday 1st November)
The castle is still in use as a family home by the Norfolk family so entry to the castle rooms is only available between the hours of 12 noon and 17.00. However, this gives you plenty of time to explore the Gardens, Chapel and Castle Keep beforehand, they open at 10am.

Please note that there is a strict no photos inside the castle rule. You can however take some brilliant photos from the top of the Castle Keep and capture the fantastic views of the local area.

With helpful guides in every room to assist you with any questions it is the perfect place to learn about the fascinating history of Arundel Castle and the Duke of Norfolk and his family.

As the castle is the Duke of Norfolk's residence, with many of the rooms still in use, the experience is made all the more enriching. The 34 foot long library is amazing and not to be missed.

The Castle Keep (open 10am until 16.30)

There are 131 steps to climb up to the Keep with the staircase occasionally getting narrow in places. Once you get to the top the views are incredible with the sea, River Arun, town and the Downs all in sight.

Fitzalen Chapel (open 10am until 17.00)

The Fitzalen Chapel is an added bonus to the visit. The atmospheric Gothic chapel, with carved stone tombs, was founded in 1390 by the 4th Earl of Arundel and to this day is still the burial place of the Dukes of Norfolk. What makes the Fitzalen Chapel quite unique in England is the glass wall that divides the Chapel from the parish church. It was decided in 1879 that the Chapel did not form part of the Protestant parish church and was to remain Catholic.

The Gardens and Grounds (open 10am until 17.00)

The 40 acres of beautiful grounds and gardens are worthy of a lengthy explore. They are a very popular part of the day for many visitors. The gardens are well laid out and perfect for all to enjoy. The 'Collector Earl's Garden' is a favourite and a relatively new addition in tribute to Thomas Howard, 14th Earl of Arundel (1585-1646), known as 'The Collector'. Other walled gardens include The Stumpery (designed using old tree stumps), English Herbaceous Borders, the Cut Flower Garden and the Organic Kitchen Garden that provide the Castle (including the restaurant) with fresh fruit, vegetables and cut flowers. Exotic fruits and vegetables can be seen in the restored lean to peach house and vinery, built in 1850 by Clarke & Hope.

Events at the Castle

It is worth checking out the website for the numerous events held at the castle throughout the year. The Jousting and Medieval Tournament Week in July is a particularly popular one where knights from around the world battle it out in the shadow of Arundel Castle, Medieval style.

Other events include Living History Days, Town Criers competition amongst other exciting occasions.

Entry to Arundel Castle

Prices

There are various combinations of ticket options, depending on what you want to see;

Bronze – Gardens & Grounds, The Collector Earl's Garden, Fitzalan Chapel, Shop, Cafe & Restaurant. £9 for adults, children and concessions.

Silver – All of the above plus the Castle Keep. £11 for adults and concessions, £9 for children.

Gold – All of the above plus Main Castle Rooms. £16 for adults, £13.50 for concessions and £9 for children (family tickets for 2 adults and 3 children £41.)

Gold Plus – All of the above plus Castle Bedrooms. £18 for adults, £15.50 for concessions and £9 for children (family tickets for 2 adults and 3 children £45.)

Season tickets and group discounts are available.

Opening Times: March 28th 2015 until November 1st 2015. Tuesdays to Sundays inclusive, Bank Holidays and August Mondays.

Dogs: Only Guide Dogs are permitted.

Parking: A Pay and Display car park opposite the castle.

Address – Arundel Castle, Arundel, West Sussex, BN18 9AB **www.arundelcastle.org** or telephone – 01903 882173

Recommended Time at Arundel Castle
Depending on which ticket you want to go for will determine how long you will spend at Arundel Castle. As will the weather too. I recommend at least 3 to 4 hours to fully appreciate everything Arundel Castle has to offer.

Eat and Drink
The Bay Tree Restaurant – Located in Arundel serving brunch, lunch, dinner or just a drink. Dine within the pretty 16th century timber building or relax on the terrace. A contemporary European menu is offered and reservations are recommended.
www.thebaytreearundel.co.uk 21 Tarrant Street, Arundel, West Sussex, BN18 9DG – 01903 883679

The Swan Pub – A traditional pub dating back to 1759. The pub has lovely riverside views and serves a great selection of classic British food. A children's menu is also available. Breakfast, lunch and dinner served, or just a refreshing drink.
www.swanarundel.co.uk 27-29 High Street, Arundel, West Sussex, BN18 9AG – 01903 882314

Saint Mary's Gate Inn – Open log fires, freshly prepared food and a warm welcome in this 16th Century Inn.
www.stmarysgate.co.uk London Road, Arundel, West Sussex, BN18 9BA – 01903 883145

In the Area
The market town of Arundel is a unique and cosmopolitan town rich in history and heritage. With antique markets, art galleries, independent shops and waterside eateries, with views over the River Arun. Arundel Cathedral is an impressive Victorian Gothic style building overlooking the town.

Feeling active? Head to the South Downs National Park for some walking, cycling or horse riding.

Getting There From London
By Car – Arundel Castle is between Worthing and Chichester on the A27. Approx. driving time from central London is 1 hour 45 minutes, depending on traffic. Mill Road Car Park is located directly opposite the castle and is pay and display.

By Train – A regular and direct train service runs between London Victoria and Arundel. The journey time takes under 1 hour 30 minutes. The castle is a 10 minute walk away, or you can catch a taxi from the station (there is a taxi rank based at the station.)

BATH

Photo Credit – VisitEngland/BathTouristPlus/Colin Hawkin

Bath is a unique, stylish and wonderful city. A designated UNESCO World Heritage site, the perfect place to explore Roman Baths, natural thermal waters, stunning architecture, Georgian terraces and much, much more. A day trip from London to Bath won't seem enough, I'm sure you will fall in love with Bath, but, hopefully with this guide you will be able to get a memorable overview of this world class tourist destination.

Money Saving Tip – A Bath Visitor Card is available for £3 offering various discounts off of attractions, restaurants and shops. It is valid for 3 weeks from first validation.

www.visitbathshop.co.uk

Things to See in Bath
Bath is a compact city and most of the attractions are within easy reach of each other.

Roman Baths Museum
The Roman Baths Museum is an absolute must when in Bath. I would recommend coming as early as you can in the day (midweek if possible) as it does get busy. The audio guide really does bring the experience to life and is available in 8 different languages, as part of your admission cost.

The complex is a well-preserved Roman site that was once used for public bathing. The actual baths are below modern day street level and include the Sacred Spring, the Roman Temple, the Roman Bath House and the Museum.

Admission – Adult £14 (£14.50 during July & August), Concessions £12.25, Child (6-16) £9, Family Ticket (2 adults and up to 4 children) £40.

Money Saving Tip – You can purchase a money saver ticket and enter the Roman Baths Museum, Fashion Museum and Victoria Art Gallery. Adult £20, Concessions £17, Child £10.75, Family Ticket £49.50

Opening – January to February 9.30am to 4.30pm (closing at 5.30pm), March to June 9am to 5pm (closing at 6pm), July to August 9am to 9pm (closing at 10pm), September to October 9am to 5pm (closing at 6pm),
November to December 9.30am to 5pm (closing at 6pm.) The Roman Baths Museum is closed on December 25th and 26th.

www.romanbaths.co.uk – telephone (24 hour info) 01225 477867 – Stall St, Bath, BA1 1LZ

The Pump Rooms

The perfect accompaniment after seeing the Roman Baths Museum would be afternoon tea (or an alternative beverage) at this beautiful restaurant, built in 1795. The Pump Room is elegant with stunning decor throughout. There is a fountain with the warm spa water flowing from it – you can even taste the water containing 43 minerals.

Assembly Rooms & the Fashion Museum

Wander around the Assembly Rooms and appreciate where the Bath socialites of the 18th century would gather to listen to music, dance, drink tea and play cards. There are 4 rooms to explore, the Ball Room, the Tea Room, the Octagon Room and a Card Room. The Assembly Rooms are also home to the Fashion Museum with its collection of world renowned dresses, including both contemporary and historic styles.

Admission – Adult £8.25, Concessions £7.25, Child (6-16) £6.25, Family ticket (2 adults & 4 children) £24. An audio guide is included in the cost of admission.

Money Saving Tip – If you are planning on visiting the Roman Baths and the Victoria Art Gallery as well you can purchase a Saver Ticket for £20 (adults), £17 (concessions), £10.75 (children) and £49.50 (family.) Even if you don't visit the Victoria Art Gallery you will make a saving on just the 2 attractions.

Opening – Open daily, but please check before your visit as the rooms are hired out as a venue so may be closed on certain days. They are closed on 25th & 26th December. They open at 10.30am every day and close at 4pm in January & February, at 5pm from March until October and 4pm in November and December.

Contact – **www.fashionmuseum.co.uk** or telephone 01225 477789
Fashion Museum, Assembly Rooms, Bennett Street, Bath BA1 2QH

Bath Abbey

VisitEngland/Bath Tourism

Bath Abbey is the last great medieval church to be built in England. The 15th century Bath Abbey was built between 1499 and 1616, with the internal fan vaulting was erected during the 19th century. Visitors can climb the 212 steps of the tower, the reward is a beautiful panoramic view of the city at the top. You are able to sit behind the face of the clock and stand on the Abbey's vaulted ceiling. This is part of a fully guided tour lasting around 45 minutes. Tower tours are closed on Sundays. Tickets cost £6 per adult and £3 per child (5 to 15.) Please book via **towertours@bathabbey.org**

Admission – It is free to enter Bath Abbey, but there is a suggested donation of £2.50 per adult (£1.50 per student) to help with the maintenance of the abbey.

Download a free audio guide before you visit – www.bathabbey.org/creatingvoices

Opening – Bath Abbey is open from 9.30am until 5.30pm on Mondays, 9am until 5.30pm from Tuesday to Friday, 9am until 6pm on Saturdays and 1pm until 2.30pm and 4.30pm until 5.30pm on Sundays.

Contact – **www.bathabbey.org**

Pulteney Bridge

VisitEngland/BathTourismPlus

A very beautiful and historic bridge lined with shops, cafes and restaurants. It was completed in 1774 by the architect Robert Adam for William Pulteney to connect central Bath with the other bank of the River Avon. The best way to view it is from the river bank which you can access via some narrow steps at the end of the bridge.

Jane Austen Centre

Jane Austen made Bath her home from 1801 to 1806 after two long visits at the end of the 18th century. Jane Austen's connections with Bath are showcased at the Jane Austen Centre in a permanent exhibition. Located in an original Georgian townhouse, costume guides will show you the links between Bath and Jane Austen and her family. Within the Jane Austen Centre are the Regency Tea Rooms, serving coffee, afternoon tea or champagne, alongside delicious scones, crumpets, cakes, sandwiches and other tasty treats.

Admission – Adult £9, Senior £8, Student £7, Child (6 to 16) £5.50 and Family (2 adults and up to 4 children) £23.

Opening – Open 7 days a week (closed 25th, 26th December and 1st January.) March until 1st November it is open from 9.45am until 5.30pm (July and August 9.30am until 6pm.) From 2nd November until 4th April it is open from 11am until 4.30pm each day apart from Saturday when it is open from 9.45am until 5.30pm.

Contact – **www.janeausten.co.uk** – The Jane Austen Centre, 40 Gay Street, Bath, BA1 2NT

Royal Crescent

Overlooking Royal Victoria Park is the splendid semi-circular terrace of Georgian houses named Royal Crescent. Built in the 18th century for the wealthy socialites of Bath. Visitors can go in No 1 Royal Crescent and learn about life during that time. The House has been furnished and decorated according to the style of 1776 – 1796.

Admission – £9 adults, £7 concessions, £4 children (6-16), Family (2 adults and up to 4 children) £22

Opening – In 2015 they are open from Sunday 1 February until Sunday 13th December. The opening hours are Tuesday-Sunday from 10.30am to 5.30pm. On Mondays they are open at 12noon until 5.30pm. Last entry is 4.30pm.

Contact – **www.no1royalcrescent.org.uk** – No. 1 Royal Crescent, Bath, BA1 2LR

The Circus

Not far away from Royal Crescent, is the Circus. There are 30 houses divided into 3 terraces, curved in a circular shape. Famous residents have included David Livingstone and Thomas Gainsborough. The architecture is stunning with a beautiful green park area in the middle.

Thermae Bath Spa

Unfortunately you can't bathe in the Roman Baths, but that is where the Thermae Bath Spa comes in! Visitors can bathe in four natural thermal baths, including the amazing open-air rooftop pool with incredible views of Bath's skyline. Over 40 complementary therapies are available in the treatment rooms alongside four state-of-the-art steam rooms.

Admission – Children under the age of 16 are not permitted. No bookings can be made for spa sessions in advance unless you are a group of 8 or more or are having a spa treatment. A 2 hour spa session costs £32 from Monday to Friday (£10 for each additional hour) and £35 on Saturdays and Sundays (£10 for each additional hour.)

Opening – Thermae Bath Spa is open every day except 25th, 26th December and 1st January. The New Royal Bath is open from 9am until 9.30pm. The Cross Bath is open from 10am until 8pm (last entry 6pm.) Included in your visit is the Open-air Rooftop Pool, the Minerva Bath, Aroma Steam Rooms and Springs Cafe & Restaurant. The weekends are the busiest times with Tuesdays, Wednesdays and Thursdays often being quieter.

Contact – www.thermaebathspa.com – Thermae Bath Spa, The Hetling Pump Room, Hot Bath Street, Bath, BA1 1SJ

Royal Victoria Park

The park was officially opened by Queen Victoria, who the park was named after, when she was just 11 years old, in 1830. Royal Victoria Park is not far from the city centre, just a short walk away. The park covers 57 acres with a wide range of activities. Highlights include an 18 hole mini golf course, botanical gardens, tennis, an adventure playground, skateboard park, BBQ facilities, a lake and a band stand with lots of musicians performing throughout the year. Stop off in the Royal Pavilion Cafe situated within the park for tea, coffee, cake or other refreshments.

Sally Lunn's

Sally Lunn's is a world famous tea and eating house and can be found in one of the oldest houses in Bath, dating back to 1482. Sally Lunn was the legendary creator of the Bath bun, a regional speciality. Whilst at the tea rooms you can actually visit the kitchen where the baker first created the bun, which has been turned into a small museum.

Visit Sally Lunn's for morning coffee, lunch, afternoon tea or dinner. Regional English food is served including their 'trencher dinner.'

www.sallylunns.co.uk – 4 North Parade Passage, Bath, BA1 1NX

Boating on the River Avon

Within walking distance of the city centre you can hire a punt, canoe, rowing boat or kayak and explore the River Avon.

Admission – Adults £7 per hour, £4 per extra hour or £18 per day. Children £3.50 per hour, £2 per extra hour or £9 all day. Concessions £7 per hour or £11 all day.

Open – Open from 3rd April until 20th September from 10am until 6pm.

Contact – www.bathboating.co.uk or telephone 01225 312900 – Forester Road, Bathwick, BA2 6QE

Tours

City Sightseeing Hop on Hop off Open Top Bus
There are 2 routes you can go on, the City Route (50 minutes) and the Skyline Route (45 minutes.)

Tours cost £14 for adults, £8.50 for children, £11.50 concessions and £39 for families (2 adults and 3 children.)

Free World Heritage Site Audio Tour
A free walking guide from Visit Bath taking you through the city's architecture and history is available for download from **www.visitbath.co.uk**

Eat and Drink

Rosarios – A traditional Italian cafe serving tasty cakes, drinks, pastries and light meals including sandwiches, paninis, salads and homemade soups. Takeaway available. A wide choice of gluten free food is available.
www.roscoff.co.uk – 18 Northumberland Place, Bath, BA1 5AR – 01225 469590

Crystal Palace Pub – Located in the centre of the city in a Grade II listed building, serving a traditional lunch and dinner menu. They serve tasty roasts on a Sunday.
www.crystalpalacepub.co.uk – 10-11 Abbey Green, Bath, BA11NW– 01225 482666

The Raven of Bath – Located on a quiet cobbled street in the centre of Bath. A traditionally family owned pub serving a brilliant range of pies with mash or chips. Other meals include Ploughman's Lunch, locally made sausages and more. Only children over the age of 14 are allowed in.
www.theravenofbath.co.uk – Queen Street, Bath – 01225 425045

The Bathwick Boatman – Set in the perfect location overlooking the River Avon serving freshly cooked delicious dishes. Closed on Mondays.
www.bathwickboatman.com – Forester Road, Bathwick, Bath, BA2 6QE – 01225 428844

The Bell Inn – A cooperative pub owned by 536 customers since July 2013. With live music, quality real ales and pub games including billiards, table football, chess and backgammon.
www.thebellinnbath.co.uk – 103 Walcot Street, Bath, BA1 5BW – 01225 460425

Getting There From London
Train – Southwestern run direct trains from London Paddington to Bath Spa. The journey time is around 1 hour 24 minutes. If you book far enough in advance, tickets can start as low as £12 each way.
www.southwesttrains.co.uk

Car – London to Bath is around 115 miles. Depending on traffic, journey time will be around 2 hour 10 minutes via the M4. There are 3 park and ride services for Bath and a number of car parks.

Coach – National Express run coaches from London to Bath. The fastest coach time is 2 hours 35 minutes (one way) with others taking around 3 hours. For cheapest fares and the best choice of departure times, please book as far in advance as you can.
www.nationalexpress.com

Organised Tour –A number of tour companies organise day trips from London to Bath. They include;

www.andersontours.co.uk – Day trip to Stonehenge and Bath with entry to Stonehenge and the Roman Baths. Adult prices are from £59 and Child prices are from £53.

www.goldentours.com – Offer a variety of tours that include Bath.

Visitor Information Centre
Abbey Chambers, Abbey Churchyard, Bath BA1 1LY – **www.visitbath.co.uk** Located next to Bath Abbey

BRIGHTON

Credit – VisitEngland/Andrew Marshall

Brighton is an exciting and vibrant city on the south coast of England. Often called 'London on Sea' it comes highly recommended as a day trip from London. One day won't cover it all and you will undoubtedly yearn to return for some more seaside fun.

Once a small fishing village with narrow winding lanes, Brighton has grown into a major visitor destination, attracting many day trippers from London. Brighton is also perfect for a city break, with events taking place all the time.

The range of things to do in Brighton is plentiful and varied. Just heading straight for the beach area and people watching is an experience not to be missed. Brighton prides itself on its uniqueness, attracting visitors, students and residents from all over the world.

The following list of things to do in Brighton is by no means complete, but is a good starting point for the day trip visitors.

Shopping in Brighton – A Shoppers Paradise

Brighton has fantastic shopping opportunities. You could spend the whole day exploring the various distinct shopping areas.

Church Hill Square – A shopping mall with all the well-known high street names.

The Lanes – A collection of little twisty narrow lanes leading to unique, diverse and independent shops. Absolutely do not miss Choccywoccydoodah – the ultimate chocolatier. Lots of jewellery and antique shops, alongside delicious restaurants and pubs.

North Laine – Over 300 independent shops within less than half a square mile. The exciting range of shops include the popular Vegetarian Shoe Shop (**www.vegetarian-shoes.co.uk**) alongside stylish studios selling local artwork, vintage boutiques, music shops, gifts and plenty of opportunities to stop off for a recharge in one of the friendly bars or cafes and soak in the buzzing atmosphere.

London Road – Located to the north of Brighton, London Road encompasses an area rich in history with a mix of independent and specialist shops. The country's oldest working cinema, The Duke of York's Picturehouse (**www.picturehouses.com**) is in the Preston Circus area, where you can step back in time and watch a movie (current, classic or independent are all available) with a glass of something from the bar.

Elsewhere in the London Road area is the home of Brighton's most famous market, the Open Market, selling local eggs, meat, cheese, fruit and veg and fresh fish. All from Sussex's best food producers. **www.brightonopenmarket.co.uk.**

Head to **www.visitlondonroad.co.uk** for a full low down on what shops are there.

Kemp Town

A laid back area just off the seafront with a mix of independent quirky shops, vintage second hand shops, cafes, pubs and bars. Kemp Town is home to most of the city's gay nightlife. I really love this part of Brighton. There are some great pubs, places to eat, with more of an emphasis on independent businesses. It is well worth an explore of this vibrant chilled out part of Brighton.

For quite possibly the best ice cream in Brighton, head to Gelateria De Luca at 107 St Jame's Street. If the taste of freshly made bread is your thing, do not miss Real Patisserie. It is served as fresh as you can get, made from beginning to end on the premises. They also freshly make a huge selection of pastries, and if you get there early enough, they might still be warm from the oven. **www.realpatisserie.co.uk** – 34 St George's Road, Kemp Town

Beach Front

On the beach, west of Brighton Pier, you will find the bohemian Artist's Quarter with a range of art studios and housed in what were once Fisherman's arches. Some beautiful artwork can be bought here and I recommend a stroll down here. Further down towards the old pier are the West Pier arches with some retail outlets selling a range of items including children's clothing, home ware and other gifts.

Royal Pavilion

A building quite unlike most others, unique and exotic, a wonder and an absolute must see. The Royal Pavilion is an incredible sight and was once the palace of Prince Regent (George IV.) When you first set eyes on it you can imagine it in India, which is the style that the prince requested the architect John Nash design it in.

From the outside the Royal Pavilion is visually stunning – and inside is equally amazing. Be prepared for your jaw to drop when you see the interior. The 'Banqueting Room' is incredible, and as for the chandelier, weighing in at a hefty 1 tonne, you just know this room is going to impress.

Adult admission costs £11.50, Children (5-15) £6.20, Concessions £9.50 and family tickets (2 adults and 2 children) costs £29.20.

Money Saving Tip – If you download the free Brighton Museums App (see www.brightonmuseums.org.uk for details) you can claim £1 off your entry. An audio tour is included in admission prices and is available in a variety of languages.

Museums
Brighton Museum and Art Gallery – In the Royal Pavilion Garden
www.brightonmuseums.org.uk

Brighton Fishing Museum – In the Fishing Quarter on the seafront
www.brightonfishingmuseum.org.uk

Old Police Cells Museum – Policing history from 1830
www.oldpolicecellsmuseum.org.uk

Brighton Toy Museum – Situated under Brighton Station, over 10,000 exhibits on display, one of the finest collections in the world.
www.brightontoymuseum.co.uk

Palace Pier
The Grade II listed building has a history dating back to 1823. It has of course seen many changes over the years, including complete rebuilds due to storm damage. If you fancy a typical fish and chip dinner, head to the famous Palm Court Restaurant on the pier. If you are taking your food away, just watch out for the persistent seagulls overhead, they have no fear and think nothing of swooping in for your portion of chips.

Elsewhere on the pier are amusement arcades with fruit machines galore, and right at the end, a fairground with dodgems, 'turbo coaster' and other typical fairground rides. Classic stalls can be found in the fairground area, including Tin Can Alley and Hook a Duck. If this all seems like too much excitement, grab yourself a deckchair and a traditional piece of Brighton Rock and watch the fascinating world of Brighton pass by.

If you happen to still be around at sunset during the winter months, you might be lucky enough to see the delightful display that the starlings like to put on. The starlings are returning to roost from across the Sussex countryside. We have been there a few times when it has happened and it is quite the sight to see!

The Beach
Brighton beach, on the English Channel, is a bustling and atmospheric area. Go for a walk along the lower promenade lined with souvenir shops, bars, cafes and art galleries. On warmer days, grab a cool drink at one of the beach side bars and soak in the cosmopolitan atmosphere surrounding you. When day turns to night, the bars and clubs open for people to party the night away under the Victorian beach front arches.

During the summer months (April to September), you can catch a ride on the **Volk's Railway**, the oldest running electric railway in the world.

Volk's Railway dates back to 1883 and has a long and interesting history. Passengers can start their ride by Brighton Aquarium on the seafront, all the way down to Brighton Marina.
www.volkselectricrailway.co.uk

There are very few traditional **Punch and Judy shows** left in the UK, once a firm favourite of visitors to seaside resorts. Children would watch in delight at the famous puppet show. Luckily, Brighton is still fortunate enough to have one of the most talented puppeteers putting on this classic British seaside event. The shows take place on the lower promenade outside the Brighton Fishing Museum.

For further show details please visit their website **www.punch-andjudy.com**

Get a panoramic view of the city on a **Brighton Wheel** voyage. Passengers can enjoy a journey 3 times round the wheel, 50 metres above sea level, in observation pods holding 6 adults and 2 children. The experience lasts 12 minutes and has a guided commentary as you go round.

Adults tickets cost £8 (£7.20 if bought online) and £6.50 for children (£5.85 if bought online.) Other tickets are available, including VIP Champagne experiences. Please see the website for more information. **www.brightonwheel.com**

Brighton Marina & Rottingdean Village

Indulge in a spot of boat watching as you stroll around the modern Brighton Marina. There is a selection of specialist shops, including home furnishings, gifts, fashion and books. Elsewhere you will find a variety of cafes and restaurants of every cuisine. The Marina is also home to a bowling alley, cinema and casino. **www.brightonmarina.co.uk**

If you fancy getting out to sea, you can take a boat or sea fishing trip. Choose a mini cruise to suit you, take in the Sussex Coastline including the West Pier, Palace Pier, or further along towards Seven Sister's Cliff and Beachy Head near Eastbourne. **www.watertours.co.uk**

From the Marina you can walk along the undercliff to Rottingdean, a picturesque seaside village. The walk is about 3 miles long with incredible views out to sea and breath taking white cliffs, with beach access for a spot of rock pooling. Keep an eye out for any fossils! Stop off for a refuel at the highly recommended Ovingdean Undercliff Cafe. Rottingdean was mentioned in the Domesday book, becoming en vogue in the 19th century amongst writers and artists. Rudyard Kipling lived here from 1897 to 1902 in a house he rented and wrote some of his famous stories, including some of the 'Just So' titles. The gardens were restored by The Rottingdean Preservation Society and opened for the public to enjoy in 1986. **www.rottingdeanpreservationsociety.org.uk**

The High Street in Rottingdean provides plenty of opportunities for refreshments, with a choice of 5 pubs and various independent tea rooms, cafes and restaurants.

Eat and Drink

Brighton Marina has many well-known restaurants to choose from including Pizza Express, Prezzo, Zizzi and other chain restaurants. For something a bit different try the Brighton Pagoda, a floating Chinese restaurant. Located in the marina, it is a great unique restaurant. **www.brightonpagoda.co.uk**

For a small village, Rottingdean has a great selection of places to stop for food and drink.

Queen Victoria – A traditional pub on the high street serving local ales, ciders and a great food menu.

The Plough Inn – Another highly recommended pub in the village serving a classic pub menu using fresh and locally sourced food. Weekends do get busy so it is worth booking for food. **www.theploughinnrottingdean.co.uk** – Vicarage Lane, Rottingdean – 01273 390635

Tours

City Sightseeing – Hop on Hop Off bus tour of Brighton starts at Brighton Pier. Get on and off at any of the stops along the route. Tickets are valid for 24 hours. The tour is in operation from April to September. Commentary is available in English, Spanish, French, German, Italian, Chinese and Japanese. The route includes the West Pier, Hove, the shopping areas of Churchill Square, North Street, Brighton Marina and back down to Brighton Pier. Tickets cost £11 for adults, £5 children, £23 for a family ticket and £8 for concessions.

Visit **www.city-sightseeing.com/tours/united-kingdom/brighton**

Brighton CityWalks – A 90 minute walking tour of historic Brighton.
www.brightoncitywalks.com

Brighton Chocolate Tour – Learn all about chocolate and the history of the city, tasting some delicious treats along the way. The tour lasts 3 hours and costs £33 for an adult ticket.
www.chocolateecstasytours.com

Brighton Sewer Tours – Yes, you did read that correctly, a sewer tour! Run by SouthernWater, this popular tour runs from May to September. A guide will take you through 366 metres of the 48km of sewers. The tours start at the Palace Pier and end through a manhole in the middle of Old Steine Gardens. Learn the fascinating history of the sewers from Victorian times. Tours last about 1 hour and must be booked in advance at **www.southernwater.co.uk**
Tickets cost £12 for adults and £6 for 11-16 year olds.

Only in Brighton – Unique walking tours of Brighton lasting 80 minutes. Be entertained as you learn some intriguing and unusual insights into the city. Adult tickets cost £8, under 14s are free, concessions £6. Tours start at 7pm outside the Royal Pavilion shop. Please see the website for tour dates and booking.
www.onlyinbrighton.co.uk

Other Tours – For a wider choice of tours including Ghost Walking Tours, Offbeat Brighton, Mods & Rockers Brighton please see the official Visit Brighton website **www.visitbrighton.com**

Brighton Events
There is always something going in in Brighton, from Foodies Festivals, the UK's biggest celebration of food and drink, to the largest arts festival in England, Brighton Fringe taking place throughout May. To list all the events would be a book in itself, so here is a just a snippet. For full listings please go to **www.visitbrighton.com/whats-on**

Brighton Pride – This year is the 25th Anniversary, so expect big celebrations. This year 1st & 2nd August 2015
www.brighton-pride.org

Brighton Fringe – One of the largest in the world. Takes place for the whole month of May
www.brightonfringe.org

Foodies Festival – A food and drink lover's perfect destination. The UK's biggest celebration of food and drink. Takes place 2nd, 3rd and 4th of May.
www.foodiesfestival.com

Artists Open Houses Festival – Around 200 artist's homes and studios open up to the public to show the work of over 1,000 artists. The largest of its kind in the UK. It is running from 2nd May until 24th May 2015.
www.aoh.org.uk/may-2015-festival-home

Mini Run –Watch as over 2,000 minis make their way from London to Brighton. This year is 17th May 2015.
www.london-to-brighton.co.uk

Veteran Car Run – Hundreds of vintage vehicles from the UK and abroad drive from London to Brighton. This year it takes place on 1st November 2015.
www.veterancarrun.com/home

In the Area

South Downs National Park – Easily accessible by bus, bike or car, the South Downs National Park has incredible views, walks and rolling hills. For ideas and inspiration on places to visit within the National Park please see **www.visitbrighton.com/countryside/the-south-downs**

A great way to get around is by bus, get a Discovery Ticket for unlimited travel for the day across the South Downs (adults £8.50, children £7 and family £16.) For maps and planning see the website **www.southdowns.gov.uk/discover/**

Alternatively, 'Breeze up to the Downs' is a network of 3 buses linking Brighton to Devil's Dyke, Ditchling Beacon and Stanmer Park. **www.brighton-hove.gov.uk**

Getting There From London

I would always recommend coming to Brighton on the train from London if you can. Driving to Brighton from London is fine until you reach the city, especially down by the seafront, where the traffic crawls at a painfully slow pace. Once you have navigated your way to a parking spot (not any easy task) you will pay a small fortune to park up for the day. The train is direct, fast and the station is not that far from the seafront.

Train – Direct trains go from London Victoria (52 mins), London Bridge (58 mins) and London St Pancreas 1 hour 16 mins.)

Car – Central London to Brighton is about 50 miles via A23/M23 and will take roughly 90 minutes, depending on traffic. As I mentioned above, parking is challenging so be prepared to drive around a bit before you find a free spot. There are plenty of multi storey car parks in the shopping areas but these can sometimes fill up, especially on weekends.

Coach – National Express go from London Victoria Coach Station to Brighton. Journey time varies but is around 2 hours 20 minutes. The coach stops at Pool Valley Coach Station

BLUEBELL RAILWAY

Photo Credit Jon Bowers

Experience the exciting bygone era of the steam train on The Bluebell Railway in Sussex. The Bluebell Railway is one of the best preserved railways in the country. The heritage line stretches for 11 miles through the beautiful Sussex Weald countryside. The Bluebell Railway Preservation Society owns the railway and do a fantastic job of raising money to restore, maintain and further improve the line, with members being mainly volunteers with a passion for the railways.

In March 2013, the railway was extended and began running to the terminus station in East Grinstead, meaning that there is now a convenient connection to Southern Railway. The locomotives operate between the stations of East Grinstead and Sheffield Park, with stops at Horsted Keynes and Kingscote. The collection owned by the society is the largest collection of steam engines in the south of the country.

The 22 mile round trip on one of the steam trains is an incredible experience, delivering some stunning views of the local area. However, the Bluebell Railway is much more than just a train ride. Each train stop along the way offers something for the visitor, both adults and children. The train ride takes about 40 minutes from beginning to end and you can get off at each stop as you wish. You can begin your journey at Sheffield Park or East Grinstead, but if you are coming by train from London it makes sense to start in East Grinstead.

The Train Stations

Sheffield Park

Originally built in 1882 for Lord Sheffield who owned and lived in a nearby estate. The station has been restored in a 1880s style by the Bluebell Railway. The Bluebell Railway Museum can be found on platform 2 at Sheffield Park where you can discover the railway's history when it first began in 1882 and follow the journey right up to the present day.

Get up close to the incredible locomotives and carriages with a visit to the locomotive shed on platform 1. You might spot the famous "Stepney" from the well-known Thomas the Tank Engine stories.

Other Facilities at Sheffield Park Station

Souvenir and gift shop.
Picnic area – pack a lunch and eat alongside the River Ouse.
Pub Lunch – eat in The Bessemer Arms at the station
Station Car Park (including disabled bays)
Toilets (including baby changing and disabled)

Attractions near Sheffield Park Station
A short walk away from the station is Sheffield Park and Garden, owned and managed by The National Trust. The estate dates back several centuries having had many different uses over the years. The 300 acres of parkland is the perfect place to explore the trails and discover woodland walks. The area is home to a wide range of wildlife including dragonflies, kingfishers, birds of prey and butterflies.

Children will love the woodland play area at Ringwood Toll where they can practice their balance on the beams, get involved in some den building or climb the log wall. The informal landscaped garden has 4 amazing lakes which make for a stunning photo opportunity. Explore the paths that surround the lakes through the glades and wooded areas.

Prices start at £9.90 for an adult entry, family tickets are available. National Trust Members go free. The Garden is open every day except Christmas Day.

You can walk to the National Trust Garden from Sheffield Park Station. There is also a bus service that links the Bluebell railway with the Garden at weekends from Easter until October.

For further details please **www.nationaltrust.org.uk/sheffield-parkand-garden**

Horsted Keynes
You may be familiar with Horsted Keynes station from the popular TV series, Downton Abbey. Built in 1882, once upon a time the station was a junction station. The Bluebell Railway have restored the station to the mid-1920s age. Visit the award winning Carriage and Wagon department where all the restoration of carriages happens. There is a viewing gallery accessible from platform 5.

Other Facilities at Horsted Keynes Station:

Station Refreshment Room – snacks, teas and coffees are available when the trains are running. Light meals are available during the school holidays and weekends
Toilets (including baby changing facilities)
Station Car Park

The Village of Horsted Keynes
Horsted Keynes is a small village with two local pubs, both serving real ales and traditional pub food. The village church, St Giles, was built over 900 years ago by the Normans. Former Prime Minister Harold Macmillan is buried in the churchyard – he had a private home (Birch Grove) in the area. American

President J.F. Kennedy stayed at Birch Grove on an overnight stay, a few months before he was assassinated in Dallas, Texas.

Kingscote
Kingscote Station was built in 1882 and restored by the Bluebell Railway to the mid-1950s era. There is a great picnic area behind platform 2 where you can watch the trains as you eat.

Other Facilities at Kingscote Station

Station Refreshment Room – Serving tea, coffee and snacks (open spring until autumn)
Toilets (disabled toilets and baby changing facilities available)

Things to do in the area
In the heart of Kingscote Valley, 2,500 acres of leisure area connected by pathways and bridleways, sits Kingscote Vineyard, a fully functioning winery, vineyard, restaurant and sales area. With 15 acres of the classic Champagne triumvirate planted so far, accompanied by a 2 acre modern planted apple orchard for creating the tasty Kingscote Sparkling English Cider. They are a 10 minute stroll away through the beautiful Gravetye Estate (or if you phone in advance they will come and pick you up.)
www.kingscotevineyards.com – 01342 327535

East Grinstead
The platform at East Grinstead for The Bluebell Railway was opened in March 2013 and has opened the line up to train visitors on the line from London. The ancient market town of East Grinstead is well worth a visit, either prior to your Bluebell ride or after. The main centre is about a 5 minute walk from the station and has all the usual high street shops alongside independent and unique shops which are worth a visit. The old high street has one of the longest runs of 14th Century timber framed buildings in the country.

The town also has a small museum documenting the history of the area, including the events of WWII. Sackville College, built in 1609, is at the far end of town where the Christmas Carol 'Good King Wenceslas' was written.

Eat & Drink in East Grinstead
East Grinstead has a number of coffee shops and restaurants in town to choose from.

Bluebell Cafe – At the top of Railway Approach you will find the Bluebell Cafe, serving a wide choice of foods including breakfasts, lunches, dinners and other snacks. I highly recommend the breakfasts!
www.bluebellscafe.com – 110-112 London Road, East Grinstead –01342 458491

CJ's Cafe Bar – Lovely both during the day and evening. With breakfast, lunch and dinner menus, delicious tapas and a selection of wines and beers. There is a pleasant rooftop terrace to sit out on during the warmer days.
www.cjs-cafebar.co.uk – 55-57 High Street, East Grinstead, RH19 3DD – 01342 301910

Other Facilities at East Grinstead Station
Booking Office
The Grinsteade Shop and Buffet Carriage, serving light snacks, teas and coffees.
Toilets
Car Park

Other Events

The Bluebell Railway frequently puts on special events throughout the year. It is worth checking on their website before you travel to see if anything is on. Events include; Diesel Weekend, Bo Beep Easter Special, Fish & Chip Specials, Rail Ale Evenings, Steam & Cream, Murder Mystery Evenings on the Golden Arrow Pullman. During certain times there are special deals on such as 'Kids for a Quid.'

Admission

Ticket prices vary so please check **www.blue-railway.com** for exact costs. At the time of writing, an adult ticket for unlimited use on the whole line for one day costs £17.

General Booking Enquiries: 01825 720800

Getting there from London

Train – the best way to get to The Bluebell Railway from London is to take a Southern Railway train from London Victoria (services run every 30 minutes.) The train takes under an hour. For train times and prices check **www.thetrainline.com**

Car – East Grinstead is about 30 miles from central London and will take about 1 hour and 10 minutes to drive. There are a number of pay and display car parks in and around the town.

CAMBRIDGE

The university city of Cambridge is steeped in rich history and tradition. Cambridge draws visitors to the city to admire the jaw dropping architecture, ancient colleges and beautiful riverside. Just wandering around the bustling, atmospheric is memorable enough.

Things to do in Cambridge

There are a total of 31 colleges within Cambridge University, but not all of them are open to the public to visit.

King's College Chapel

The incredible looking King's College Chapel took over a century to build. It was begun in 1446 by Henry VI and is a stunning example of late Gothic architecture. One of its claims to fame is the largest fan vault ceiling in the world. The medieval stained glass windows telling the story of the bible are equally stunning.

I really recommend trying to be there at Evensong which takes place at 5pm from Monday to Saturday and 10.30am and 3.30pm on a Sunday. Not only do you get to enter for free, you also get to experience the goose bump inducing choir. It is a magical experience.

Entry – Adult tickets cost £8, Children and Concessions £5.50.
Opening – During term time it is open from 9.30am until 3.30pm Monday to Friday, 9.30am until 3.15pm on Saturdays and 1.15pm until 2.30pm on Sundays. Out of term time it is open 7 days a week from 9.30am until 4.30pm. Please check the website for term time dates and any other closures **www.kings.cam.ac.uk/visit**

Trinity College & the Wren Library

A fantastic Cambridge landmark dating back to the 13th century. The house of Isaac Newton is a spectacular site that you really should try and see when in Cambridge. Winne the Pooh fans will enjoy being able to read A A Milne's manuscript which is held here in the Wren Library within Trinity College. Henry VIII founded Trinity College in 1546, visitors can see the Great Court, Nevile's Court and the Ante-Chapel. The Wren Library where A A Milne's manuscript can be found, was designed by the well-known architect, Christopher Wren. There are four statues on the roof representing the studies of Divinity, Law, Physics and Mathematics.

Other works contained within the Wren Library include 1250 medieval scripts, many books from Sir Isaac Newton's own library and the Capell collection of early Shakespeare editions. The Wren is open to visitors at certain times of the year. It is usually open from 12 noon until 2pm Monday to Friday and on Saturday mornings in Full Term from 10.30am until 12.30pm. Numbers are restricted to 15 people at a time and photography is not allowed.

Admission – Entry to the Wren Library is usually free. A small charge of £2 per adult and £1 per child to enter Trinity College.
Opening – Various times and days, please see the website for the latest information.
Contact – **www.trin.cam.ac.uk** – Trinity College, CB2 1TQ – 01223 338 400

The Centre for Computing History

A unique museum with a huge range of computers from decades past. With interactive activities and many of the computers working, you are able to use them and some of the games to find out (or remember!) how computers have evolved over the years. A great trip down memory lane for many.

Open from Wednesday to Sunday from 10am until 5pm. The cost of entry is £7 for adults, £5 for children (5-16), a family ticket (2 adults and 2 children) costs £20.

www.computinghistory.org.uk – Rene Court, Coldhams Road, Cambridge, CB1 3EW – 0844 357 5100

Punting on the River Cam

VisitEngland/Iain Lewis

If you want to try punting, Cambridge is absolutely the place to do it. Not only is it a really fun activity, it is also a great way to see some of the colleges and bridges from an alternative viewpoint known as 'The Backs.'

Whether you are brave enough to do it yourself, or hire a chauffeur, is entirely up to you. The benefit of a chauffeur, aside from the obvious point of being able to sit back and relax instead of navigating, is that your tour guide will be able to inform you about the history of the River Cam and surrounding area.

There are a number of tour companies offering punting. Try Let's Go Punting who offer a selection of tours including private, group, evening tours and wine tasting. Shared tours cost £16 for adults (£12 if booked online), Concessions £14 (£10 if booked online), Children £8 (£7 if bought online.) **www.letsgopunting.co.uk**

An alternative option is Scudamore's Punting Company **www.scudamores.com**

Cambridge American Cemetery and Memorial
A short distance from Cambridge is the American Cemetery. It is spread over 30 acres of perfectly manicured hillside to commemorate the 3812 American service men and women who lost their lives during World War II in Britain. There is a Wall of Remembrance with the names of 5127 soldiers engraved on it, those that have no final resting place. It is a very peaceful and moving place to visit, well worth the detour if you can. Most of those that died did so during the Battle of the Atlantic or the strategic air bombardment of northwest Europe.

In May 2014 a new visitor centre was opened with interactive displays, photographs, films and personal stories to help visitors understand the importance of the campaign.

It is open, together with the visitor centre for the public to visit. Opening hours are 9am until 5pm daily, except December 25th and January 1st when it is closed. During opening hours there is a member of staff available to answer any questions and escort relatives to grave and memorial sites.

The Cambridge American Cemetery is located about 3 miles out of Cambridge. The City Sightseeing Tour (mentioned below) stops here on its hop on hop off loop.
madingleyamericancemetery.info – Cambridge American Cemetery, Coton, Cambridge, CB23 7PH – 01954 210 350

Church of St Mary the Great
A lovely church next to Kings College. The physical foundations of Great St Mary's date back to around 1010. Written records show that a church has existed since 1205, 10 years before the Magna Carta was signed. A real highlight of visiting the church is the trip up the tower. Although a small fee is payable to climb it, the views of the surrounding colleges and countryside is not to be missed. The spiral staircase that leads up is quite narrow.
www.gsm.cam.ac.uk – St Mary's Passage, King's Parade, Cambridge, CB2 3PQ – 01223 741720

The Fitzwilliam Museum
One of Cambridge's best known museums and one of the finest small museums in the world. With a wide range of 30 exhibits over 2 main floors. The museum is very well laid out with works from Salvador Dali, Poussin, Gainsborough, Degas and many more. Entry is free but a donation is welcome.

The museum is closed on Mondays and open from 10am until 5pm Tuesday to Saturday. Sundays and Bank Holidays it is open from 12 noon until 5pm.
www.fitzmuseum.cam.ac.uk – Trumpington Street, Cambridge, CB2 1RB – 01223 332900

Tours in Cambridge

Cambridge Tour Guides – Offering a variety of walking tours of Cambridge
www.cambridgetourguide.co.uk

City Sightseeing – Get around Cambridge on the hop on hop off tour bus. Stopping at 20 stops throughout the city as well as the American Cemetery. Adult tickets cost £14.50, Children £8.50, Concessions £11.50 and a family ticket (2 adults and 3 children) £36.
www.city-sightseeing.com

Eat and Drink

The Eagle – A traditional pub whose origins date back to 1525, making it one of the oldest in Cambridge. Reportedly the location where Crick and Watson announced their discovery of DNA, during one of their daily lunchtime drinks. The historic pub was also used by RAF and the US 8th Air Force pilots during WW2 with lots of their names and squadron numbers written on the ceiling.
www.eagle-cambridge.co.uk – 8 Benet Street, Cambridge, CB2 3QN

The Maypole – A traditional pub with a high focus on quality, not only with service, but also with food and drink. Serving tasty Italian dishes alongside traditional English food. With many ales, ciders and frequent beer festivals.
www.maypolefreehouse.co.uk – 20a Portugal Place, Cambridge, CB5 8AF – 01223 352999

The Urban Shed – Offering an incredible range of sandwiches, milkshake, coffee and breakfasts. Closed on Wednesdays.
www.theurbanshed.com – 62-64 King Street, Cambridge, CB1 1LN – 01223 324888

Fitzbillies – A popular and well known bakery and café serving delicious pastries and other savoury foods. It is open for coffee, cake and afternoon tea 7 days a week. Dinner is served from 6pm on Thursdays, Fridays and Saturdays. Try one of the famous sticky chelsea buns that have been made on the premises since 1921.
www.fitzbillies.com – Trumpington Street, Cambridge, CB2 1RG – 01223 352500

In the Area

Anglesey Abbey – A National Trust owned Jacobean-style house with gardens and a working mill, 7 miles east of Cambridge.
www.nationaltrust.org.uk/anglesey-abbey – Quy Road, Lode, Cambridge, Cambridgeshire, CB25 9EJ

Getting There From London

Train – Direct trains from London Kings Cross (46 mins), London Liverpool Street (1hr 20) going to Cambridge Station. The actual train station isn't as close to the city centre as other places, so look out for the Citi1, Citi 3 and Citi 7 services from the station to the centre. If you would rather walk it will take about 30 minutes.

Car – It is about 60 miles from central London to Cambridge. Journey time should be about 90 minutes on the M11. There are 5 Park and Ride sites on the outskirts of the city that offer parking and a frequent bus ride into the centre. If you are coming from the M11 the best place would be the Trumpington one (CB2 9FT.) At the time of writing bus tickets cost £2.70 per person with up to 3 children travelling free.
www.cambridgeshire.gov.uk

CANTERBURY

Canterbury is the perfect day trip from London, incorporating ancient ruins, culture, history and of course the oldest cathedral in England. The history of Canterbury sits well alongside a modern day, vibrant city, with independent shops, first class restaurants and inviting pubs.

Getting around Canterbury is easily done on foot, with plenty of organised or self-guided tours available. Mix your day up with a combination of exploring the ancient UNESCO World Heritage Sites with a relaxing boat trip along the River Stour.

What to see in Canterbury

Canterbury Cathedral

Photo Credit – VisitEngland/VisitKent

Taking centre stage along Canterbury's skyline is Canterbury Cathedral, a World Heritage Site, dating back to 597AD. The beautiful Cathedral is a stunning building and a must see attraction whilst you are in Canterbury. The impressive Cathedral is steeped in history with the Archbishop Thomas Becket having been murdered here in 1170. See where he was murdered and visit his former resting place.

You will feel a real sense of awe as you enter the building, with incredible architecture spanning the centuries. The medieval stain glass windows are breath taking, especially if you are lucky enough to be there on a sunny day when the windows will display in all their beautiful glory. The staff and guides within the Cathedral are both helpful and knowledgeable. If you are able to take a tour it is worth doing for the extra insight to the Cathedral. But, if you can't, just wandering around and soaking in the ambiance of your surroundings will be a magical experience.

There is a lot to see in the Cathedral so allow at least 2 hours to fully appreciate both inside and the gardens. Guided tours are available for an extra cost, they take about 90 minutes.

Opening – The Cathedral is used frequently for services and events so double check on the website to make sure it is open when you visit. The Cathedral is open from 9am until 5.30pm from Monday to Saturday (open until 5pm in the winter months), and 12.30 until 2.30pm on Sundays.
Admission – Adults entry is £10.50, Concessions £9.50, Children (5-18 years) £7.

Money Saving Tip – If you are travelling by train to Canterbury you can use a 2 for 1 entry voucher. Register here for your voucher
www.visitkentoffers.co.uk/2-for-1-offers

Money Saving Tip – Download this voucher for free child entry (one child free per paying adult.)
www.canterbury-cathedral.org

St Augustine's Abbey
Many visitors miss seeing the fascinating and peaceful site of St Augustine's Abbey. Located outside the city walls, it is also part of the Canterbury World Heritage Site. The abbey was founded shortly after 597AD to mark the rebirth of Christianity in Southern England. As well as the ruins of the abbey, there is also a museum and a free audio tour.

Opening – From March to September the abbey is open 7 days a week, 10am until 6pm. Please check here for winter opening times **www.english-heritage.org.uk/visit/places**
St Augustine's Abbey, Longport, Canterbury, Kent, CT1 1PF.
Admission – Adults £5.40, Child (5-15) £3.20, Concession £4.90,
Family (2 adults, 3 children) £14.

Money Saving Tip – If you are an English Heritage member, entry is free. Please see our chapter on '**Passes and Discounts**' to find out more details.

St Martin's Church
The oldest practicing Anglican Church in the English speaking world, built in 540AD. It is a small and atmospheric church steeped in fascinating history, it is where St Augustin started the conversion of England to Christianity in 595AD.

Opening – Only open on certain days of the week so check on the website. Current opening times are Tuesday, Thursday and Saturday 11am to 3pm, Sundays 9.50am to 10.20am.
North Holmes Road, Canterbury, CT1 1PW. The church is about a 10 minute walk from the city centre.
www.martinpaul.org Entry is free

Westgate Towers
An iconic and distinctive landmark in Canterbury, Westgate Towers stands beside the River Stour. Once upon a time, medieval pilgrims would pass under the 60 foot high gatehouse arch on their way to visit the shrine of Thomas Becket at Canterbury Cathedral. It is the largest surviving city gate in England.

Westgate Gardens
Located next to Westgate Towers, a highlight of Canterbury, Westgate Gardens is a brilliant place to escape for some tranquillity. Westgate Gardens is ideal for a picnic, with 11 acres of public gardens along

the banks of the River Stour. The gardens have been a public space since the Middle Ages so come with their own history. Highlights include the 200 year old and 25 foot wide Oriental Plane Tree, the Norman archway and other medieval ruins.
www.westgateparks.co.uk

Canterbury Roman Museum

This small museum will give you an interesting insight to Roman life in and around Canterbury. The Roman Museum is underground, built around the remains of a Roman town house. The museum has plenty of displays and an area for children to dress up as Romans and handle some of the items on display. A highlight includes the remains of a Roman mosaic pavement. Allow up to an hour to fully explore the museum. Guided tours are available at an extra cost.

Opening: The museum is open all year, closing on Christmas Day, Boxing Day and New Year's Day. Opening hours are 10am until 5pm, last entry 4.15pm.
Admission: Adult tickets cost £8, Concessions £6, Children are free (maximum of 2 children per paying adult.)

Money Saving Tip – Buy a joint Heritage and Roman Museum ticket for £10 (for 2 adults) and £8 (for 2 concessions)

Money Saving Tip – If travelling by train or bus to Canterbury you can use a 2 for 1 entry voucher. Register here to download your voucher **www.visitkentoffers.co.uk/2-for-1-offers**

The entrance is close to the Cathedral on Butchery Lane. **www.canterbury-museum.co.uk**

Canterbury Heritage Museum

A unique museum telling the story of Canterbury, set within a magnificent medieval building. Highlights of the museum include the childhood classics Bagpuss, Rupert Bear, the Clangers, Ivor the Engine alongside The Canterbury Cross, The Poor Priests Hospital, Oliver Postgate's story of Thomas Becket amongst other fascinating exhibits showcasing Canterbury's past.

Opening: Opening hours vary so please check on the website before planning this attraction. **www.canterbury.co.uk/museums** Stour Street, Canterbury CT1 2NR

Admission: Adults £8, Concessions £6, Children are free (to a maximum of 2 per each paying adult)

Money Saving Tip – Buy a joint Heritage and Roman Museum ticket for £10 (for 2 adults) and £8 (for 2 concessions)

The Beaney House of Art & Knowledge

A quirky little museum that is free to enter. Highlights include a bug collection, Enid Blyton section and a mummified cat! There is lots of local information and changing exhibitions. **www.canterbury.co.uk/beaney/**

The Canterbury Tales

Dedicated to this well-known piece of English Literature, The Canterbury Tales attraction will take you through the collection of the famous medieval tales. Introduced by costume characters and with a handheld audio guide you will become immersed within the recreation of five of Chaucer's most loved tales. A fun way to learn about one of the great classics. Allow about 45 minutes to see Chaucer and his Pilgrims.

Opening – The Canterbury Tales is open daily apart from Christmas Day, Boxing Day and New Year's Day. Opening hours are Jan/Feb 10am until 4.30pm, March-June 10am until 5pm, July/August 9.30am until 5pm, September/October 10am until 5pm, November/December 10am until 4.30pm.
Address – The Canterbury Tales, St Margaret's Street, Canterbury, Kent, CT1 2TG
Admission – Adults £8.95, Child £6.95 (ages 5-15), Concessions £7.95, Family (2 adults, 2 children) £27.75

Money Saving Tip – Book online for discounts

Money Saving Tip – If you are visiting Canterbury by bus or train you can use a 2 for 1 entry voucher. Download it here **www.visitkentoffers.co.uk/2-for-1-offers/**

Canterbury Historic River Tours
A unique way to see parts of the city that cannot be seen on foot. The River Stour flows through the heart of historic Canterbury. Canterbury Historic River Tours dates back to 1932, so even they have a history! The round trip takes about 40 minutes. Highlights of the tour include; Kings Bridge, Eastbridge Hospital, Franciscan Island, Greyfriars Chapel, Old Weavers House, Kings Mill, Alchemist Tower, Cromwellian Forge, Friars Bridge, Blackfriars, Dominican Priories, The Abbots Mill, The Marlowe Theatre and the Ducking Stool.

Opening – The season runs from March 1st until November 10th with tours leaving every 15 to 20 minutes between 10am and 5pm.

Canterbury Historic River Tours, Kings Bridge, Canterbury, CT1 2AT **www.canterburyrivertours.co.uk** **enquiries@canterburyrivertours.co.uk** or 07790 534744

Admission – Return tickets cost £8.50 for adults, Concession £7.50, Child (up to 12) £5, Child (12-16) £5.50, Family (2 adults and 2 children) £23.

Walking Tour
Canterbury Guided Tours offer daily tours of the city including the Cathedral precincts, King's School, the Pilgrim Inns around the medieval lanes with tales of various famous historical characters, writers and artists. The tour lasts about 90 minutes and takes you through the world famous historic streets of Canterbury.

Opening – Open every day apart from Christmas Day. Tours start at 11am throughout the year and twice a day at 11am and 2pm from 1st April until 31st October.
Christ Church Gate, The Precincts, Canterbury, Kent, CT1 2EE **www.canterburyguidedtours.com** **guides@canterburytouristguides.co.uk** or telephone on 01227 459779.

Admission – £7.50 for adults, £5.50 for children (under 12), £7 concessions, Family Ticket (2 adults and children) £25. You can book online or at Canterbury Visitor Centre, the Roman Museum or at the Beaney in the High Street.

In the Area
Chilham Village – A small and sweet quintessential English village a short drive (7 miles) from Canterbury. If you are driving from London it is worth the detour. A picture perfect place with brilliant pubs and shops, a 15th century church and a great tearoom for some tasty scones, jam and clotted cream.

Whitstable – The popular seaside town of Whitstable is 7 miles away, accessible by car (20 mins), train (Canterbury East to Whitstable via Faversham, 29 minutes) or bus (Stagecoach East Kent buses from Canterbury Bus Station, taking approx. 35 minutes.) For full details please see the Whitstable chapter.

Getting There From London

Train – Trains leave from London Victoria for Canterbury East (direct 1hr29), London St Pancras Intl for Canterbury West (direct 59 minutes), and London Charing Cross for Canterbury West (direct 1hr 38). The
Cathedral and the other attractions are an easy walk from either station.

Car – Central London is about 60 miles from Canterbury and takes about 1 hour 40 to drive via the M2 and A2. For car parks and park and ride schemes in and around Canterbury please see this information **www.canterbury.gov.uk**

Coach – National Express run coaches from London Victoria Coach Station to Canterbury, the fastest taking about 1hr45.

CHISLEHURST CAVES

Chislehurst Caves are not far from central London. Located close to Bromley in Kent, 30 metres deep, lay 22 miles of passageways that although called caves, were dug by man and once used as chalk and flint mines.

The only way to explore the caves is on a guided tour which lasts about 45 minutes. With the aid of a handheld lantern, you will be led through the mysterious tunnels by your guide who will explain the fascinating history of Chislehurst Caves, from the days of the Druids and Romans up to more recent rock concerts that took place within the caves. They have had many uses over the years, as a shelter during World War II, a music venue which saw the likes of David Bowie, Status Quo, Jimi Hendrix, The Rolling Stones and Pink Floyd all perform there.

The caves are also said to be haunted – find out more during your tour! There is also a gift shop and cafe.

TIP – Dress appropriately, it is noticeably cooler in the caves so take a jumper at least. There are some uneven floor surfaces so wear appropriate footwear.

Admission – Adult prices are £6, children and senior citizens £4

Money Saving Tip – Chislehurst Caves is an attraction within the London Pass.

Opening – Open from Wednesday until Sunday. Guided tours start at 10am and run every hour on the hour with the last one starting at 4pm. During local school holidays and bank holidays the caves and cafe are open daily, apart from Christmas and New Year.
www.chislehurst-caves.co.uk – Caveside Close, Old Hill, Chislehurst, Kent, BR7 5NL – tel: 020 8467 3264

In The Area
Down House – Visit the home of Charles Darwin just 6 miles away (about 20 minutes in the car.) See the house and garden where he thought about and developed many of his theories. Down House is an English Heritage managed site and costs £10.60 to enter (adults), £6.30 (children), £9.50 concessions and £27.50 for a family ticket (2 adults and 3 children.) See the chapter at the beginning on **passes & discounts** for details on the English Heritage Pass.
www.english-heritage.org.uk

Getting There From London
Train – South-eastern trains run from London Charing Cross and London Cannon Street. They take just under 30 minutes to get to Chislehurst train station. The caves are a short 5 minute walk from the station.
Car – Chislehurst Caves are about 13 miles from central London and the drive time should take about 1 hour via the A21, depending on traffic. There is free parking at the caves.

COLCHESTER

Colchester is Britain's oldest recorded town, attracting over 4.5 million visitors each year. Colchester has a rich history dating back 2,000 years. In 2004, Britain's only Roman Circus was discovered in the south of the town.

Colchester Castle Museum

Photo Credit – VisitEngland/VisitEssex

Colchester Castle was built when Colchester was the first Roman capital of Britain, it was built even before the Tower of London. It is the largest Norman Keep in Europe. The museum has plenty of interactive and hands on activities to explain the history and heritage of the castle to visitors. The Castle is one of the most important heritage sites in England, showcasing a large collection of Roman finds of national and international interest.

Colchester Castle Museum is brilliant for children with opportunities to dress up and experience being inside a replica thatched roundhouse. Throughout the year the museum offers a variety of events for visitors to take part in, including tours, talks, quizzes and workshops.

For an extra charge, you can book a tour that takes you up onto the Castle roof, offering fantastic panoramic views of the town, and then down into the Roman vaults.

You can enrich your experience with the Castle App. Available for hire are tablets with the App preloaded on it, at a cost of £1. The App recreates how the Castle would have looked back in the day.

Entry to the Castle

Adult tickets cost £7.50, Children (ages 4-16) and concessions £4.75, Family and saver tickets are available for £19.75 (please see the website for details on eligibility.) The tour to the roof and vaults costs an additional £2.80 for adults and £1.40 for children.

The Castle Museum is open Monday to Saturday 10am to 5pm, Sunday 11am to 5pm

Further Information

Colchester Castle, Castle Park, High Street, Colchester, CO1 1TJ Telephone 01206 282939
www.cimuseums.org.uk/castle

Castle Park

Colchester Castle is set in the pretty Victorian Castle Park, having a Grade II listing in the English Register of Parks and Gardens of Special Historic Importance. The park stretches across 11 hectares, divided by the Roman Wall that crosses through it. There is plenty to do within the park, aside from the Castle Museum, there is a boating lake, play park, cafe, crazy golf, a band stand, First Site Art Gallery, the Natural History Museum, Minories Art Gallery and Hollytrees Museum.
www.colchestercastlepark.co.uk

Museums & Galleries

The Natural History Museum is free to enter with hands on activities to learn about the local natural environment.

Another museum with free entry is **Hollytrees Museum**, a stunning Georgian building displaying family life and childhood in Colchester over the past 300 years. Learn about life before washing machines, enjoy the miniature world of the Hollytrees dolls house and discover the origins of Twinkle Twinkle Little Star! Follow the story around this beautiful Georgian building taking in domestic life and childhood in Colchester over the past 300 years.

The Minories Art Gallery and Firstsite (located in a distinctive golden building) are both contemporary art galleries and are free to enter. Firstsite (**www.firstsite.uk.net**) offers a wide-ranging programme of creative events and activities for the whole family. The Minories Art Gallery (**www.colchester.ac.uk**) offers varied exhibits in a lovely Georgian building. Enjoy a coffee and slice of cake in the beautiful and relaxing garden.

Colchester Town Centre

The town has a great selection of shops, restaurants, bars and cafes. Colchester has a fantastic mix of high street names alongside smaller independent shops situated down quiet lanes.

Colchester Guided Tour

A great way to learn about the history of Colchester is to go on a guided walking tour led by a qualified Town Guide. The 90 minute tour leads you through Castle Park, the Dutch Quarter and the High Street. Learn about why Boudica destroyed the Roman Temple of Claudius, the origins of Twinkle Twinkle Little Star, when Colchester was under siege for 11 weeks, and more fascinating history from Colchester's rich past. Call 01206 282920 or email **vic@colchester.gov.uk** for bookings and further information.

In the Area

Layer Marney Tower

VisitEngland/VisitEssex

Built during the reign of Henry VIII, Layer Marney Tower is England's tallest Tudor Gatehouse. Layer Marney Tower is still a family home but visitors can come and enjoy the tower and grounds. Climb the 99 steps to the top of the tower, the reward being magnificent views on a clear day. The gardens are beautiful and children will enjoy the farm animals and Wildlife Walk.

As it is still in use as a family home, please double check the opening times. Currently, during the summer season, it is open on Sundays and Wednesdays from 12 noon until 5pm.

Entry costs £7 per adult, £4.50 per child and £20 for a family ticket (2 adults and 2 children.) **www.layermarneytower.co.uk** – Layer Marney Tower, Nr Colchester, Essex, CO5 9US

Tiptree Jam Museum

Are you a jam lover? If you are driving, you could make a divert to Tiptree Jam Museum on the way there or back. The museum is free to enter where you can learn about the history of the village and how the art of preserve making has developed over the years. Of course, you should treat yourself to a well-deserved 'Tiptree' Strawberry Conserve with home-made scones and fresh cream, served with the 'Tiptree' tea of your choice.

Tiptree Tea Room, Wilkin & Sons Limited, Tiptree, Essex, CO5 0RF Tel: 01621 814524 **www.trooms.com** tiptree@trooms.com

Getting There From London

Train – Direct trains leave from London Liverpool Street to Colchester Station, taking around 45 minutes.

Car – Colchester is about 65 miles from central London. If you take the A12 route through Chelmsford it should take you around 1hr and 30 minutes. Colchester has a new Park & Ride service. It is located north of junction 28 of the A12. Currently the service is available Monday to Saturday (closed Sundays and Bank Holidays) between 7am and 7pm.

EASTBOURNE

The seaside resort of Eastbourne, with a pebbly beach and clean promenade, makes for a welcome break from the hustle and bustle of the capital. Elegant hotels line the seafront with the colourful Carpet Gardens in front. At the western end of Eastbourne seafront is the famous Beachy Head with its high chalk sea cliffs. They are part of the South Downs National Park and Seven Sisters Country Park and make for a great side trip from the beach front.

What to see in Eastbourne

The Seafront

Photo Credit – VisitEngland/Visit Eastbourne

Eastbourne beaches are clean and welcoming. The award winning blue flag beaches offer clean waters to swim in (when the weather allows) and are easily accessible. There are a choice of beaches with Grand Parade Beach being the main one by the pier. There are showers, toilets, lifeguards, first aid, refreshments and beach hut hire available.

Our favourite beach in Eastbourne is Holywell Retreat, at the foot of the South Downs. It is always easy to find beach front parking, even on hot days. Access to Holywell is down a steep winding hill (remember you will need to walk back up it, so what goes down, must be carried back up!) At the bottom you will find a lovely cafe (Holywell Tea Rooms) serving delicious refreshments and food. There are also toilet facilities. This area is where the Dotto Train turns around to make its journey back along the seafront to the Marina. You are able to hop on and off at various stops along the way, making it a great way to see the whole seafront with some great views along the way.

If you manage to coincide your stay at Holywell beach with the tide going out, it is the perfect place to go rock pooling with large expanses of sand also being revealed. Check tide times here **www.tidetimes.org.uk**

When at Holywell, if you walk a little further west (away from the main resort of Eastbourne), you will find the Holywell, a well at the foot of the cliffs where fresh spring water comes out.

If you head east of the pier you will come across the Redoubt and Harbour Reach beaches heading towards the marina. By the Redoubt beach is Redoubt Fortress and Eastbourne Heritage Service. Redoubt Fortress is a historic landmark dating back over 200 years. It was built to protect the South Coast from Napoleon – today it is home to the largest military collection in the south of England. Entry to the actual fortress and Parade Ground is free with a small fee charged for entry to the museum (£4.50 adults, £3.25 concessions, £2.50 children and £12 for up to 5 family members.) Lots of events are put on throughout the year. **www.eastbournemuseums.co.uk**

Sadly, in July 2014 a fire occurred on Eastbourne Pier, destroying the main roof which dated back to the 1870's. Fortunately the pier was safely evacuated and nobody was hurt. The pier is now reopened following extensive restoration work, with more work still taking place.

The pier offers some good views of the town and has the usual pier facilities including refreshment outlets, shops and several benches to just sit back and enjoy the seaside.

Along the seafront, not far from the pier, is Eastbourne Bandstand. The bandstand is well maintained and used regularly for events including tribute acts, Prom concerts, kid's concerts and 1812 Firework concerts. Tickets can be bought online or on the night, where available. **www.eastbournebandstand.co.uk**

Sovereign Harbour Marina

The marina is a pleasant and quiet marina to wander about, admiring the boats coming and going. There are a selection of restaurants and cafes to stop off for food and refreshments. The marina is a stop on the Dotto Train mentioned earlier in the chapter. It is located at the far eastern side of the Pier.

Beachy Head

Photo Credit – VisitEngland/Visit Eastbourne

The highest chalk cliffs in Britain, standing at 162 metres above sea level. On a clear day, the views from the top are stunning across the English Channel. On a windy day, pack an extra layer or two, it gets a bit breezy up there! Call in to the Beachy Head Countryside Centre and see the free Download Experience, an exhibition showing the history of the Downs and Beachy Head. There is a shop within the centre selling gifts and maps of the area.

At the top, you can stop for a picnic or head to the Beachy Head Inn serving meals and snacks. There are numerous walks that can be done from here. A good one to start with is the Beachy Head walk, a 90 minute circular walk taking in Birling Gap. For a full list of suggested walks and routes **www.beachyhead.org.uk**

Getting to Beachy Head

Car – You can drive up to Beachy Head and park in the large public pay and display car park. From Eastbourne Pier, drive along the sea front with the sea on your left. You will pass St Bede's Prep School on your left. Follow the road up the hill and then the signs to Beachy Head.

Walk – Walk up from the foot of Beachy Head below (past Holywell and St Bede's Prep School.)

Bus/Tour – The hop on hop off bus also takes you up to the top of Beachy Head (covered later on in the chapter.) The 13X Coaster Tourist Trail Bus takes you to Beachy Head from Eastbourne Pier. It also goes onwards to Birling Gap, Seven Sisters Country Park and Brighton. One day Discovery fares are available, allowing you to explore the area by bus in an economical way. Adult fares are £8.50, Child (5-15) £7 and a Family Discovery is £16. **www.buses.co.uk**

Boat – Or, for an alternative view, take a boat trip to the iconic Beachy Head lighthouse from the Sovereign Marina. The 1 hour long boat trip takes you along the seafront of Eastbourne, past the pier and Holywell and on to the famous white cliffs and the iconic light house. A knowledgeable guide will tell you about the maritime heritage and geology of the coast.
www.sussexvoyages.co.uk

Tours of Eastbourne

City Sightseeing – A great way to get around Eastbourne is on the hop on hop off open top bus. With 23 stops to get on and off at including Eastbourne Pier, the Bandstand, Beachy Head (the foot of), Beach Head (the top), Birling Gap and the Marina, the round trip takes about 60 minutes with buses coming every 30 minutes. A commentary in English is available aboard the bus. The tour bus runs from 21st March until 25th October 2015. Tickets cost £10 for adults, £7 for children and concessions and £32 for families (2 adults and 3 children.)
www.city-sightseeing.com

Birling Gap

Part of the world famous Seven Sisters chalk cliffs, Birling Gap makes up one of the longest stretches of undeveloped coastline along the south coast of England. Birling Gap is run by the National Trust who have a cafe, shop and visitor centre on the cliff top. The views from the cliff tops of the Seven Sisters are incredible, so don't forget your camera! The dramatic landscape and never ending sea is really rather breath taking. You can climb down the steps (be careful, they are steep) to the beach below with lots of areas perfect for rock pooling and picnics.
www.nationaltrust.org.uk

Getting to Birling Gap from Eastbourne

Car – Birling Gap is 5 miles west of Eastbourne. It is signposted from East Dean on the A259. Parking is available at Birling Gap for £2 for half a day and £4 for a whole day. Parking is free for National Trust Members.
Bus – The hop on hop off bus also takes you up to Birling Gap (covered earlier on in the chapter.) The 13X Coaster Tourist Trail Bus takes you to Birling Gap from Eastbourne Pier. It also goes onwards to Seven Sisters Country Park and Brighton. One day Discovery fares are available, allowing you to explore the area by bus in an economical way. Adult fares are £8.50, Child (5-15) £7 and a Family Discovery is £16.
www.buses.co.uk

Seven Sisters Country Park
A great easy walk is along the mile long track beach trail, through Seven Sisters Country Park, following the Cuckmere River. The track will take you to the shingle beach which is ideal for a picnic whilst you admire the amazing white cliffs. www.sevensisters.org.uk

Once you've completed the 2 mile round trip, The Cuckmere Inn not far from the car parks, serves great food and drinks with fantastic views. If you want eat it might be an idea to book ahead at busy times as it is a popular spot.
www.vintageinn.co.uk – Exceat Bridge, Seaford, East Sussex, BN25 4AB

Getting to Seven Sisters from Eastbourne

Car – The car park at the start of the walk is about 15 miles from Eastbourne and should take no longer than 15 minutes to drive it via the A259. The postcode is BN25 4AD. There are two pay and display car parks.

Bus – The 13X Coaster Tourist Trail Bus takes you to Seven Sisters from Eastbourne Pier. It also goes onwards to Brighton. One day Discovery fares are available, allowing you to explore the area by bus in an economical way. Adult fares are £8.50, Child (5-15) £7 and a Family Discovery is £16. **www.buses.co.uk**

Eating & Drinking in Eastbourne

The Green Almond – A popular and well-priced vegetarian restaurant offering buffet lunches 5 days a week (Tuesday – Saturday) and dinner menus twice a week (Friday and Saturday evenings.) **www.thegreenalmond.com** – 12 Grand Hotel Buildings, Compton St, Eastbourne BN21 4EJ

Dolphin Fish Bar – If you come to the seaside then fish and chips are tradition! The Dolphin Fish Bar is not far from the seafront and serves tasty fish and chips to eat either in or takeaway. **www.dolphinfishbar.com** – 86 Seaside Eastbourne, Eastbourne

The Crown and Anchor – A friendly pub with great beer available, including guest ales and a wide selection of food choices available between 12 noon and 9pm.OnSundays food is available all day including Sunday Roasts. Breakfast is served from 11am until 3pm on weekdays and 11am until 6pm on weekends. **www.crownandanchoreastbourne.co.uk** – 15-16 Marine Parade, Eastbourne BN21 3DX

In the Area

Middle Farm – If travelling by car from London (via the A27) Middle Farm makes for a great stop off. They have a fantastic farm shop stocking over 80 British cheeses and an incredible selection of meats, including 20 different varieties of sausages. Also popular with visitors is the cider and perry tasting, from a range of over 100 different draught ciders and perries. The fresh apple juice which is pressed daily is also delicious!

The farm shop and cider tasting is open from 9.30am until 5.30pm from Monday to Sunday. It is free to enter the shop and cider tasting but you must pay to enter the Open Farm (£4 per head.) Free parking is available. **www.middlefarm.com** – Middle Farm, Firle, Lewes, East Sussex, BN8 6LJ

Getting to Eastbourne from London

Car – Eastbourne is about 75 miles from central London with a journey time of just under 2 hours via the A27/M23. There are plenty of parking spaces in Eastbourne, mainly in pay and display. If you head to the seafront you will find pay and display parking bays on the street and within car parks.

Train – Southern Railway have direct trains going from London Victoria directly to Eastbourne and take just under 90 minutes. As with other lines remember, the further in advance you book, the cheaper your ticket will be! The station is about a 10 minute walk from the seafront. **www.southernrailway.com**

Coach – National Express run coaches from London Victoria Coach Station to Eastbourne. The fastest journey time is 2 hours and 50 minutes. Tickets start at £6.90 each way if booked far enough in advance.

GROOMBRIDGE PLACE

Groombridge Place offers a truly magical experience for all the family. Located in the village of Groombridge, just 4 miles from the unique town of Royal Tunbridge Wells in Kent. With award winning gardens to enjoy, and an Enchanted Forest to roam around in, everyone will have a magical time, where imaginations can run wild.

The Formal Gardens

The pretty walled gardens are complimented by the grandeur of the 17th century moated manor house, set in the background. Jane Austen's Pride and Prejudice (starring Keira Knightley) was in fact filmed at Groombridge Place in 2005. Almost a century prior to that, Groombridge Place was the inspiration for the writer Sir Arthur Conan Doyle, who created the famous character of Sherlock Holmes. A tiny museum dedicated to Sir Arthur Conan Doyle can be found amongst the 17th Century Formal Gardens.

Elsewhere within the gardens you will find the Giant Chessboard, a small maze, the restaurant and an array of colourful and lively gardens.

The Knot Garden – If you come in spring you will be treated to a beautiful display of tulips. It is from here that you will discover the door to **The Secret Garden**, a cute little hidden space where the stream meets the moat.

The White Rose Garden – With over 20 types of white rose, the White Rose Garden commemorates the 200 year old ownership of the estate by the Waller family. Other formal gardens include The Paradise Walk, The Oriental Garden, The Drunken Garden (a favourite place of Sir Arthur Conan Doyle) and The Draughtsman's Lawn. As you wonder around the gardens keep an eye out for the resident peacocks who like to strut their stuff as they roam around.

The Enchanted Forest

A world of unique and magical surprises awaits as you enter the Enchanted Forest. A canal boat can be taken to get you to Crusoe's World, (although not a necessity, it is easily walkable), it is an enjoyable ride for only £1.50 (adult) and £1 (child).

Crusoe's World is the perfect place for adventure and imagination. Based on the TV series Crusoe, the original props have been reconstructed at Groombridge Place. With several platforms at different levels, two tree houses are linked together with rope bridges and a central viewing tower.

If you can drag the kids away from this area, there are plenty of other places to discover as you make your way through the ancient woodland. The Giant Swing Trees are very popular with *both* the kids and adults! Several swings can be found, suspended from the really tall trees. Other delights waiting to be discovered include the fort, totem pole, authentic tipis and Romany caravans.

A highlight of the Forest Adventure is the 700 metre long board walk, made up of tunnels, bridges, obstacles and a zip wire. As you make your way around, see if you can spot any of the resident animals; goats, sheep, chickens, alpacas and the very unique and world famous Zedonk. If you've never heard of a Zedonk before, it is half donkey and half zebra. You will adore the stripy legs of the Zedonk!

Birds of Prey
Flying displays take place twice a day at 12.30 and 3.30pm (depending on the weather,) showcasing some stunning birds, including hawks, owls, eagles and falcons. The Raptor Centre is the largest conservation centre for birds of prey in the South East of England.

Entry to Groombridge Place

Off Peak Prices: £8.95 per adult, £7.45 Senior Citizen, £7.45 per child (3-12 years) and a family ticket costs £29.95 (2 adults and 2 children.)
Peak Prices: £9.95 per adult, £8.45 Senior Citizen, £8.45 per child (3-12 years) and a family ticket costs £33.95 (2 adults and 2 children.)
Season tickets and group discounts are available.
Opening Times: 9.30am until 5.30pm during peak time (last entry 4pm) and 10am until 4.30pm during off peak time (last entry 3pm).
Dogs: Only Guide Dogs are permitted.
Parking: A visitor car park is available.

Further Information
Groombridge Place, Groombridge Hill, Groombridge, Tunbridge Wells, Kent TN3 9QG **www.GroombridgePlace.com** 01892 861444

Recommended Time at Groombridge Place
Allow at least 3 hours to fully appreciate both the Formal Gardens and Enchanted Forest. On warm days you can easily spend much longer, fully appreciating the grounds and experiences in the forest.

In the Area
Take a ride on The Spa Valley Railway Steam train, a 10 minute walk away. Please check their website for combination tickets and timetables **www.spavalleyrailway.co.uk**

Combine with a visit to the charming and historic town of Royal Tunbridge Wells. Tunbridge Wells can be reached on The Spa Valley Railway Steam train. The town has been attracting visitors for over 400 years, perfect as either a day trip in its own right, or combined with another attraction such as Groombridge Place, or further on to the coast (perhaps Hastings.)

The popularity of the town as a royal holiday destination began when the Chalybeate Spring was discovered over 400 years ago. The historic spa town of Royal Tunbridge Wells is home to a wide range of independent and unique shops. Dining in the town is recommended with a great selection to choose from, including the Michelin-starred Thackerays. Found in the Pantiles, the Chalybeate Spring was discovered in 1606, over 400 years ago. The word 'chalybeate' means iron rich and the iron taste is obvious in the water. The spring was discovered by a Dudley North Lord when he sought out some water the morning after an overindulgent night. The spring water made him feel so much better than he declared that the spring water contained health benefits to all that drunk it. A glass of the water was then drunk each morning by visitors who came from London and elsewhere. Today, in the summer months, you can still take a drink of the water from Easter to September from Wednesday to Sunday and on Bank Holidays, between the hours of 10am and 3pm. Costs £1 each.

The High Rocks via the Spa Valley Steam Railway

Catch the steam train from the main train station to The High Rocks for a spot of rock climbing or a tasty lunch. The High Rocks is a restaurant/pub in a beautiful setting. Named after the incredible high rocks in the area, once a stone-age camp, now a National Monument. The rocks date back millions of years offering acres of amazing sandstone rocks, joined by 11 bridges, allowing a scenic walk through the peaceful woodland setting.

Alternatively you can drive to The High Rocks from Tunbridge Wells (about a 5 minute drive.) See the High Rocks website if you require more information.

Getting There From London

By Car – Approximately 50 miles from central London. From the M25 exit at Junction 5 and head south on the A21. After 10 miles, exit at A26 signed Tunbridge Wells. Take the A264 to East Grinstead and follow signs to Groombridge village and Groombridge Place.

By Train – Catch the train at London Charing Cross which run frequently throughout the day, taking under an hour to reach Tunbridge Wells. At Tunbridge Wells take a bus (no.291) or a taxi (approx. 10 minute journey time) to take you to Groombridge Place. Or have a ride on the Spa Valley Steam train (01892 537715 for times and prices.) The Spa Valley Steam train runs from Tunbridge Wells to Groombridge Station. The Spa Valley departure point in Tunbridge Wells is a 10 minute walk from Tunbridge Wells train station. It is a good opportunity to take in some of the Pantiles area of Tunbridge Wells as you make your way between the two points. From Groombridge Station is about a 10 minute walk to Groombridge Place (half a mile away.)
www.spavalleyrailway.co.uk

HAMPTON COURT PALACE

Photo Credit – VisitEngland/HRP

Hampton Court Palace is high up on many visitor's lists when they come to England. And with good reason, Hampton Court Palace is rich in atmosphere with history oozing at every turn. From the outside, it is breathtakingly beautiful, and the inside is spectacular, with fantastic exhibitions that really transport you back in time. Hampton Court Palace is mostly known as the palace of King Henry VIII, where he furnished it with luxury tapestries, paintings and furniture. The story of Henry VIII's political and marital life is a fascinating one, and being within what was once his home really brings the past to life.

Later on at the end of the 17th century, the baroque buildings were commissioned by William III and Mary II, adding the elegance and romance to the palace. The palace is set in acres of parkland and formal gardens, which are stunning in their own right. The gardens are perfectly landscaped and the trees are spectacular with some of them over 500 years old.

Costumed characters roam throughout the palace and grounds, re-enacting scenes from years gone by with singing and dancing. A useful audio tour is included with the admission price, guiding you round the Palace and providing you with interesting information about the history of Hampton Court.

Highlights of Hampton Court Palace

– Young Henry VIII Exhibition. Learn about Henry VIII as a young man and how his life changed as he got older.
– Chapel Royal. A truly beautiful chapel that has been in continuous use for 450 years. The replica crown is on display here in the Royal Pew.

– **Tudor Kitchens.** The kitchens are massive, made to feed 600 people twice a day. Live Tudor cookery events take place, check the website for what's on when.
– **Georgian Chocolate Kitchen**. A very special place, it is the only royal chocolate kitchen in Britain. It was built around 1689 for William and Mary. You can learn all about the story of chocolate in England and how it was made.
– **The Great Hall.** The largest medieval hall in England. It is also one of the oldest theatres in Britain. The walls are adorned with breathtakingly huge tapestries.
– **Cumberland Art Gallery.** Admire work from the Royal Collection, with paintings by Rembrandt, Caravaggio, Holbein, van Dyck and Canaletto.
– **William III's State Apartments & Private Apartments.** See where William III spent his time from 1689 to 1702.
– **Hampton Court Maze.** Commissioned by William III around 1700 and covering a third of an acre, Hampton Court Maze is world famous. It is probably one of the most popular attractions in the gardens with lots of people testing their sense of direction as they try to make it to the middle. Apparently the average time for getting to the middle is 20 minutes. I took 25 minutes, but then again, I'm always getting lost! Let me know what your time was and we'll see who is the fastest...
– **Hampton Court Gardens.** There are over 60 acres of stunning gardens to explore at Hampton Court Palace. Discover the water fountains, beautiful flowers and 750 acres of royal parkland. Visit the Great Vine, dating back to 1768, and said to be the longest grape vine in the world. Other highlights include The Rose Garden, Home Park with its 750 acres of deer park and ponds, the Kitchen Garden and the Royal Tennis Courts.

Entry

Money Saving Tip – Hampton Court is part of the London Pass. At the time of writing it is also part of the 2 for 1 offers with National Rail (you must travel by train to claim this offer.) Please download the voucher from **www.daysoutguide.co.uk**

Ticket prices for **1st March – 31st October 2015** are £19.30 adults (£18.20 online), Children under 16 years (under 5s are free) £9.70 (£9.10 online), Concessions £16 (£14.90 online), Family (2 adults and 3 children) are £48.20 (£44.90 online.)

Ticket prices for the rest of the year are slightly discounted. You can also just buy tickets for the maze only, or the gardens only. If you can book online do so, it will save queuing when you get there if it is a busy time (and of course save you money!)

Hampton Court Palace, East Molesey, Surrey, KT8 9AU – **www.hrp.org.uk**

Recommended Time
At least 3 hours to see everything, but if you are short on time you can still see parts of it and have a great time.

Getting There From London
Riverboat – You can catch a boat in the summer (April to October) from either Westminster, Richmond-upon-Thames or Kingston-upon- Thames. Be warned though, journeys can take up to 3 hours from Westminster, depending on the tide.
Train – Direct trains go from London Waterloo to Hampton Court (if you have an Oyster Card you can use it for this journey as Hampton Court is in Zone 6.) It takes about 35 minutes. The palace is a short walk over a bridge from the station.
Car – There is a car park, which is payable by the hour. The price per hour is currently £1.50/£1.60. The parking is limited though so be prepared on busy days to find elsewhere. The distance is about 15 miles and the journey time will be about 45 minutes, depending on traffic.

HIGHCLERE CASTLE (DOWNTON ABBEY)

© Highclere Castle LLP 2014.

If you are a fan of the award-winning TV series Downton Abbey it is possible to visit some of the locations used in the show. Depending on what you want to see, you might consider taking an organised tour to make the most of your day. Set in Berkshire in South East England, Highclere Castle is the real castle that plays Downton Abbey. It is a Victorian manor that is also home to the Earl and Countess of Carnarvon.

It has been the family home since 1679, and the author of Downton Abbey, Julian Fellowes, has been a family friend for quite some time and had Highclere in mind when writing the series. Highclere Castle is only open to the public during certain times of the year so a check with their website for current dates is an absolute must.

Tickets to enter Highclere Castle also get booked up very far in advance (at the time of writing this guide they were booked up for the whole of 2015.) They do sometimes have on the day tickets available but they are available on a first come first served basis. An alternative option might be to try and get in on one of the organised tours (if they have availability) listed further down.

Admission
– Castle, Exhibition & Gardens: Adults £20, Concession £18, Child (4-16) £12.50, Family (2 adults, 3 children) £55
– Castle and Gardens: Adults £13, Concessions £11.50, Child £8, Family £35
– Exhibition and Gardens: Adults £13, Concessions £11.50, Child £8, Family £35

– Gardens only: Adults £5, Concessions £5, Child £1.

Highclere Castle, Highclere Park, Newbury, RG20 9RN **www.highclerecastle.co.uk** **theoffice@highclerecastle.co.uk** or 01635 253210 or the 24 hour information line is 01635 253204

Opening Times – Due to the limited opening times I would advise you to check the website or call the information line before travelling.

Currently Highclere Castle is open on the following dates; 24th, 25th and 26th May, June 5th (special tour) and then for the summer Sunday July 12th to Thursday September 10th (closed Fridays and Saturdays.)

Getting to Highclere Castle from London

Train – Direct trains go from London Paddington to Newbury (the nearest train station to Highclere Castle.) A taxi can be taken to Highclere from the station, which should take about 15 minutes and about £15 each way.
Car – Highclere Castle is just under 70 miles away from central London. The journey time is about 1 hour 20 minutes via the M4. There is a carpark at Highclere Castle.
Tour – Please see below for companies offering tours for Downton Abbey.

Take an Organised Tour of Downton Abbey Sites

Brit Movie Tours **www.britmovietours.com**
Premier Tours **www.premiumtours.co.uk**
International Friends **www.internationalfriends.co.uk**

THE MAKING OF HARRY POTTER

Uncover film making Secrets at Warner Bros. Studio Tour London – The Making of Harry Potter Warner Bros. Studio Tour London offers visitors the unique opportunity to step onto the authentic sets, discover the magic behind spellbinding special effects and explore the behind-the-scenes secrets of the Harry Potter film series.

Visitors are able to walk into the original Great Hall, first built for Harry Potter and the Philosopher's Stone in 2000, experience green screen technology and marvel at the breath taking miniature scale model of Hogwarts Castle. In addition to the Great Hall, some of the most iconic sets featured in the attraction include Dumbledore's office, the wizarding shopping street Diagon Alley, the Ministry of Magic, number four, Privet Drive, Gryffindor common room and Malfoy Manor.

Newly opened in March 2015 is the must-see Platform 9 ¾ including the original Hogwarts Express steam train. You can climb aboard the train and have your photo taken with a luggage trolley as it disappears through the platform wall.

Tickets
Tickets must be pre-booked and can be purchased at www.wbstudiotour.co.uk or by calling the Studio Tour's Visitor Services Team on 0845 084 0900. Tickets book up quite quickly for busy periods so make sure you leave plenty of time to purchase.

Adult tickets cost £33, Children (5 to 15 years) £25.50. Family tickets (2 adults and 2 children or 1 adult and 3 children) are £101. There is an optional digital guide that you can hire for £4.95 (group discounts available), available in 9 languages.

Warner Bros. Studio Tour London, Studio Tour Drive, Leavesden, WD25 7LR **www.wbstudiotour.co.uk**

Recommended Time
Anywhere from 3 to 5 hours.

Getting There From London
Located just 20 miles from central London, the Studio Tour is based at Warner Bros. Studios Leavesden; the production home of all eight films. A free on-site car park is available for visitors travelling by road.

Trains run regularly from London Euston to the Studio Tour's nearest train station, Watford Junction (train time is about 20 minutes depending on which train you catch, return tickets start at £10.60 for an adult off peak). Shuttle buses are provided from Watford Junction for ticket holders with a journey time of 15 minutes.

Alternatively, you can prearrange a transfer from central London with Golden Tours. They offer a ticket and transfer package (£232 for 2 adults and 2 children) or just a transfer option (£108 for 2 adults and 2 children.) **www.goldentours.com**

HEVER CASTLE

Built in the 13th century and home to Anne Boleyn, Hever Castle is now a popular tourist attraction. Having been bought by William Waldorf Astor in the early 20th century, the castle has been renovated extensively and is in a splendid condition throughout. The Castle is set in the rural village of Hever, near Edenbridge in Kent, 30 miles from central London.

Anne Boleyn was the second wife of King Henry VIII of England. Anne Boleyn spent her younger years living at Hever Castle and two of her prayer books, complete with inscriptions and signature can be seen on display in the Book of Hour Room. It is thought that one of the prayer books is the one that Anne Boleyn had at her execution at the Tower.

The charming castle exudes splendour, with a rich and intriguing 700 year history, sure to draw in the young, old and everybody in between.

The Castle
The castle contains a selection of beautiful panelled rooms, spread over three floors, filled with antique furniture, tapestries and an impressive collection of Tudor paintings. The rooms include The Inner Hall (the Great Kitchen during Tudor times), The Drawing Room, The Dining Hall, The Entrance Hall, The Library, The Morning Room, Anne Boleyn's Bedroom, The Book of Hours Room (where Anne Boleyn's prayer books are on display), The Queen's Chamber (displaying a great collection of Tudor paintings), The Staircase Gallery, King Henry VIII's Bedchamber, The Waldergrave Room and The Long Gallery.

There is a permanent exhibition portraying the life of Anne Boleyn, both as a child at Hever Castle and her later life at the castle.

The Gatehouse is the last part of the tour, containing a collection of sinister looking instruments of torture and execution, together with historic swords and armour.

Allow at least 1 hour to explore the Castle.

Tours within the Castle
Although each room within the Castle displays useful information boards, if you want to enrich the experience with an insightful tour, the following options are available;

Castle Multimedia Guide – a 45 minute long guide is available for £3.75 each. The guide is offered in English, French, German, Dutch, Russian and Chinese. A guide for children is also available (in English.)
The guide will take you through the Castle rooms, offering a unique insight into Tudor life. Learn more about Anne Boleyn and her courtship with Henry VIII. The tour also details how the American millionaire William Waldorf Astor restored the castle.
Private Guided Tour – take an hour long tour with a knowledgeable Castle Guide. Bring the 700 year old history to life, learning all about those who lived and worked at Hever. Private tours start at 10am and 1030am and must be booked in advance (available in English, French, German, Dutch, Spanish or Italian.) Guided tours must be booked in advance.
Trails for Younger Children – these can be downloaded free of charge here. www.hevercastle.co.uk/visit/hever-castle/tours-and-trails/

The Gardens
Outside the Castle itself are the beautiful award-winning gardens, found within the 125 acres of stunning grounds that surround Hever Castle. Highlights include; The Tudor Garden, Anne Boleyn's Walk, Blue Corner, English Rose Garden (Hever Castle even has its own 'Hever Rose'), Italian Garden, amongst other glorious areas.
In addition to the splendid gardens, you will also discover plenty of wildlife within the grounds. Keep an eye out for owls, blue tits, robins, woodpeckers, kingfishers, swans, ducks, fish and insects.

Tours within the Gardens

Tours are available as part of an organised group. They last about an hour and are led by one of the knowledgeable Hever Castle gardening team. Please visit the Hever Castle website for details of the latest prices. Garden Tours need to be booked in advance. Alternatively there are plenty of trails you can choose from and download here. **www.hevercastle.co.uk/visit/gardens/tours-trails/**

Allow at least 1.5 hours to fully appreciate the gardens.

The Lake

The impressive 38 acre lake was the inspiration of William Waldorf Astor and was completed in July 1906. It took 800 men 2 years to create the tranquil lake, and now provides visitors with the opportunity to enjoy the lakeside walks and boating activities available. The lake offers some fantastic photo opportunities; whether from your peaceful walk around the lake (taking about 1 hour) or from one of the boating activities.

Activities Available

Lake Walk – Take an hour to walk around the lake and enjoy the wildlife on the way. Download the nature trail from the website if you wish to complete it. www.hevercastle.co.uk/hever-attractions/hever-lake/lakewalk/

Hire a Boat – take out a rowing boat, canoe or pedalo and enjoy the peaceful lake at your own leisure. Get a closer view of the Japanese tea house built on the edge of the lake. Please check the website for opening times throughout the year, prices and age restrictions.

Take a trip on The African Queen Steamboat – Sit back and enjoy the 20 minute leisurely trip around the lake and fully appreciate the wonderful views (£6 for an adult and £4.50 for a child.)

Other Activities at Hever Castle

There are plenty of other fun and inspiring activities available at Hever Castle throughout the year. Experiences include;

Archery and Shield Painting – Available between February and November at the weekends and during school holidays. The ancient sport is suitable for children and adults. Please allow at least 30 minutes. Payment must be made by cash, with prices starting at £3 for 5 arrows. Shield Painting is also available next to the archery, between March and November.

Jousting – A very popular event at Hever Castle, held throughout the summer holidays. The event takes place in an authentic arena where visitors can watch the Knights of Royal England compete against each other. The tournament starts with a procession from the Castle forecourt where Henry VIII and Anne Boleyn lead people to the spectacular Jousting Arena. The event is thrilling as knights duel against each other, sometimes on horseback. An excellent experience for all the family.

The Mazes – Everyone loves the challenge (and sometimes frustration!) of a maze. Hever Castle has 3 mazes; the 100 year old Yew Maze (with over a quarter of a mile of pathways), the fun Water Maze where participants must get to the centre without getting wet (hint, you will get wet, whether you want to or not!) The third maze is the Tower Maze, located in the play park, testing your knowledge on Tudor history (ages 7-14). Some of the mazes are weather permitting.

Wooden Playground – suitable for children up to the age of 14 years. A selection of swings, zip wire, slides, a large wooden climbing frame and the Tower Maze.

Miniature Model House Collection – a collection of miniature houses to show the development of English country houses through the ages. The unique houses are 1/12 scale models including The Medieval House, The Stuart House, The Restoration Drawing Room, The Georgian House and The Victorian House.

Entry to Hever Castle

Tickets can be bought on the day at Hever Castle. To save some money book your tickets beforehand (not on the day of visit though). Annual membership is available and if you are likely to at least 3 times in one year, it is worth the investment.

There are a choice of two tickets;

Castle and Gardens Ticket – £16 adults, £14 senior, £13.50 student, £9 child (5-15) and a family ticket £42.50

Gardens Only Ticket – £13.50 adults, £12 senior, £11.50 student, £8.50 child (5-15) and a family ticket £37.00

Dogs on a lead are allowed in the grounds of Hever Castle.

Opening Times

Early spring: Only open on Wednesdays to Sundays, with the Gardens open from 10.30am until 16.30 and the Castle from 12 noon until 16.30.
Main Season (March 28th until October 23rd): Open daily with the closing time extended until 18.00.
Winter Season (October 24th until November 1st): Open daily until 16.30
Winter Season (November 4th until November 27th): Open Wednesdays to Sundays until 16.30
Christmas Period: Times not available at the time of publish. Please check on the website.

Hever Castle & Gardens, Hever, Edenbridge, Kent TN8 7NG **www.hevercastle.co.uk**

Recommended Time at Hever Castle

This is very much dependent on whether you want to include entry to the Castle in your visit, and what activities you are interested in. The time of year you visit will also decide on the length of time you stay. For both the Castle and the Gardens allow at least 2.5 hours – on a nice day and if you are taking part in other activities (Lake Walk, Boating, Archery, Jousting etc.) then you could spend much longer, especially if you bring a picnic to enjoy in the grounds.

Getting There From London

By Car – Approximately 30 miles from central London. From the M25 exit at Junction 5 or 6 where it is signposted. Hever Castle is 3 miles southeast of Edenbridge off the B2026 between Sevenoaks and East Grinstead in the village of Hever. Parking is available for free.
By Train – You can catch a train from either London Bridge or London Victoria to Edenbridge Town Station. Then take a taxi to the Castle, 3 miles away. It is advisable to book a taxi in advance (Edenbridge Cars 01732 864009). Or carry on to the next station, Hever Station, and walk for 1 mile to get to the Castle. Please be advised that there are no taxis and the station is unmanned.

For a map of the walk from Hever Station to Hever Castle it is best to use the one provided by Hever Castle **www.hevercastle.co.uk/interactive-map/**

HUNDRED ACRE WOOD - HOME OF WINNIE THE POOH & FRIENDS

"You can't stay in your corner of the Forest waiting for others to come to you. You have to go to them sometimes." – Winnie the Pooh

Pooh Bear has won the hearts of millions around the world, young and old. Hundred Acre Wood, the home of Winnie the Pooh and his friends, is based on and inspired by Ashdown Forest in Sussex. The 6,500 acre woodland and heathland is the perfect place for Pooh fans to come and immerse themselves in the magic and enchantment of the area that A.A Milne called home.

A.A Milne named Pooh after a soft toy of his son, Christopher Robin Milne. Whether you are a child or an adult, you can't help but adore this lovable bear and the adventures he has with his friends. Ashdown Forest has plenty of fantastic walks to go on, with countless opportunities to spot wildlife and of course, all the locations from the Winnie the Pooh stories. There are stunning views with endless photo opportunities, picnic areas and walking trails. Ashdown Forest is a beautiful ancient forest where visitors can enjoy the simplicity of being outdoors.

I really recommend you visit Hartfield Village, home to Pooh Corner, a lovely little tea room and shop, dedicated to all things Pooh. You can purchase Winnie the Pooh souvenirs including pictures, illustrations and other items. The staff are very friendly and helpful, with maps and advice on where to go. The cafe is highly recommended, with a brilliant Pooh inspired menu, selling lots of delicious food and snacks.
www.pooh-country.co.uk

Many visitors head to Pooh Bridge, made famous in the stories by the Pooh Sticks game. If you can take your own sticks down, found earlier on, I would. Due to the popularity of the bridge and the games, sticks are in short supply! There is a free car park at the top of Pooh Bridge, although it is big, it can get busy in the summer.

Other spots to find are the Heffalumps Trap, Roo's Sandy Pit, Galleon's Lap, Where the North Pole was and maybe, just maybe, you might spy Eeyore, Tigger, Roo, Piglet or even Pooh himself.

Don't forget to find Pooh's house, knock on his door and see if anyone is home. No doubt he'll be off in search of one of his friends, or quite likely, a jar of honey.

Pooh Tours in Pooh Country

Pooh Tours provide a 5 hour guided tour of the area. All you need to do is get yourself from London to East Grinstead train station (direct trains from London Victoria are under an hour.) You will board the Bluebell Railway from East Grinstead to Sheffield Park (see our **Bluebell Railway chapter**.) After the 50 minute journey on the steam train, through the Sussex countryside, your guide will meet you at Sheffield Park where you will travel by private minibus to the Enchanted Place in Ashdown Forest.

You will go on a 2 mile guided walk through Pooh Country with a knowledgeable local guide. There will of course be a Poohsticks Championship Games, with prizes.

A picnic and afternoon tea at Pooh Corner is included in your tour. Your guide will then drive you back to East Grinstead train station for your return journey to London.

Tours cost £99 per person. Please see **www.poohtours.com** for more information and booking details.

In the Area

Depending on how long you intend to spend in Ashdown Forest will decide if you have time to visit any other places. Here are some suggestions and ideas for what else is close by. Some might be more suitable if you are driving. All these distances are from Pooh Corner in Hartfield.

• **The Bluebell Railway** (East Grinstead) is 8 miles away.
• **Groombridge Place** is 4.5 miles away.

• **Royal Tunbridge Wells** is 8 miles away.
• **Hever Castle & Gardens** is 7 miles away.
• The south coast destinations of **Eastbourne** and **Brighton** are about 30 miles further south, so you could feasibly continue on to either of these places after your visit to Ashdown Forest.

Getting to Ashdown Forest

Train – There are 3 train stations to choose from, near Ashdown Forest. Each one will require either a bus from the station or a taxi ride. Trains from London Bridge go to Crowborough, 6 miles away, with a train journey time of approx. 1hr5. Trains from London Bridge go to Uckfield, 5 miles away, train journey time approx. 1hr20. Trains run from London Victoria to East Grinstead and take under an hour. Ashdown Forest (Information Centre) is 11 miles away, with bus number 261 running from just outside East Grinstead station to the Ashdown Forest. Please check the bus timetable (**www.compass-travel.co.uk**) as buses are not very frequent. The bus journey time is approx. 20 minutes.

Car – Ashdown Forest is about 40 miles south of central London via the A22 past East Grinstead, with an approx. drive time of 1 hour and 40 minutes. There are numerous car parks dotted around Ashdown Forest. I would recommend that you either head for Pooh Corner in Hartfield (TN7 4AE) or Ashdown Forest Centre (RH18 5JP) for maps and directions.

KEW GARDENS

Photo Credit – VisitEngland/Royal Botanic Gardens, Kew/A. McRobb

Kew Gardens close proximity to central London makes it a perfect day trip contender, and is one of London's top tourist attractions.

There is always something to enjoy, no matter the season, but to make a whole day out of it, any time between spring and autumn is ideal.

Kew Gardens was originally established in 1759 and today has the world's largest collection of living plants. In 2003, Kew Gardens was made a World Heritage Site with UNESCO. Aside from the incredible collection of plants, Kew is also home to two historic buildings, Kew Palace and Queen Charlotte's Cottage.

An interesting fact – Kew Gardens has its own police force too, the Kew Constabulary, who have been in operation since 1847.

TIP – Wear layers if you can, it can get quite hot and humid in the glasshouses so you might want to take a layer off.

Things to do at Kew Gardens

There are many attractions to see and enjoy at Kew Gardens, it is a huge place (121 hectare gardens) and as I mentioned earlier, you can easily spend a whole day there. Here are some of the highlights;

Palm House

By far the most famous and iconic of the glasshouses, Palm House was designed in the 1840's by Decimus Barton and engineered by Richard Tanner. Built out of wrought iron, it was the first of its kind, created to house the exotic palms being brought to Europe in the early Victorian times.

The humid interior accommodates most known palm species and in the basement is a brilliant tropical aquarium, highlighting the importance of marine plants. You can even wear some 3d glasses and 'swim with the plankton.'

Kew Palace and the Royal Kitchens

Photo Credit – VisitEngland/Royal Botanic Gardens, Kew/A. McRobb

Built in 1631 as the home of Samuel and Catherine Fortrey, and later as a Royal residence for Queen Caroline and King George II. Kew Palace is more known as the place where King George III stayed during his 'madness.' In 1818, Queen Charlotte died at Kew Palace and the Royal Kitchens remained unused for over 200 years. They have recently been opened to visitors for the first time and offer a fascinating insight into life at Kew Palace.

The rooms in the palace have been restored in a Georgian style with some of the original furniture still there. Don't miss Princess Elizabeth's doll's house.

Admission – This is included in the admission for Kew Gardens.

Opening – Open from 2 April 2015 until 31st September 2015 from 10.30am until 5.30pm (last admission 5pm.)

Queen Charlotte's Cottage

Located near the Conservation Area, the cottage was built for Queen Charlotte, the wife of George III. It was used as a retreat in a peaceful part of Kew Gardens.

Opening – Open at weekends and Bank Holidays from April to September.

The Pagoda

VisitEngland/Royal Botanic Gardens, Kew/A. McRobb

Completed in 1762, the iconic eight-sided, ten story, Chinese Pagoda stands at an impressive 163ft tall and was designed by the architect William Chambers.

The Princess of Wales Conservatory
With 10 different climatic zones. See if you can spot the world's largest flower or some Venus flytraps.

Treetop Walkway
Designed to sway in the wind, the Treetop Walkway will provide some superb views, just make sure you've got the head for it! Designed by the same architects who designed the London Eye, the Treetop Walkway stands 18 metres tall and is 200 metres long. An explore along the walkway will give visitors the opportunity to admire the trees, birds, insects and other interesting finds along the way, all close up.

The Temperate House
The largest Victorian glasshouse in the world is currently closed for important restoration work. It is due to reopen in 2018.

Tours at Kew Gardens

Kew Explorer Land Train

The land train leaves from opposite the Victoria Gate. The hop-on/hop-off land train takes you around Kew Gardens, allowing you to get off at various stops along the way. Tickets cost £4.50 for an adult and £1.50 for a child. Tickets can be bought online or on the day.

Walking Tour

A number of free walking tours operate throughout the day, taken by enthusiastic volunteer guides. The 'Introduction to the Gardens' tour leaves at 11am and 1.30pm and the 'Themed' (variety of seasonal tours) leave at 12pm.

Admission – Adult £16.50 (with donation,) £15 standard, £14 online. Concession £15.50 (with donation), £14 standard, £13 online. Child (4-16) £3.50 at the gate or £2.50 online. Various family tickets are available.

Money Saving Tip 1
Book online for savings and fast track entry.

Money Saving Tip 2
Get 2 for 1 entry when you travel by train, download a voucher here **www.daysoutguide.co.uk/royal-botanic-gardens-kew**

Money Saving Tip 3
Kew Gardens is part of the London Pass, so entry is included if you have purchased this pass, as it fast track entry. **www.londonpass.com**

Opening – 22nd April until 31st August – Open daily from 10am until 6.30pm Monday to Friday, 10am until 7.30pm at weekends and bank holidays (Kew Palace closes at 5.30pm.) 1st September until 24th October 10am until 6pm. 25th October until 5th February 10am until 4pm. Closed Christmas Eve and Christmas Day.

Kew, Richmond, Surrey, TW9 3AB **www.kew.org**

Eating and Drinking at Kew Gardens
There are four places to eat and drink within Kew Gardens.

Outside of Kew Gardens there are a selection of cafes, pubs and restaurants, all in walking distance.

The Greyhound – Set in a great location on Kew Green, just a 5 minute walk from Kew Gardens. Serving a variety of menus including brunch, lunch and dinner. Outside there are plenty of places to sit, including some 'pods' where you can enjoy your own private TV screen, heater and service button. You need never leave your seat!

82 Kew Green, Richmond, TW9 3AP - 0208 332 9666 – **www.thegreyhoundkew.co.uk**

The Petal Pusher – A lovely welcoming place to go for breakfast, lunch or just a drink. Homemade foods, licensed restaurant, a pleasant garden and a flower shop at the back.

235 Sandcombe Road, Kew, TW9 2EW – 0208 287 1651 – **www.thepetalpusher.co.uk**

Getting There From London

Train/Tube – This is the easiest way to get to Kew Gardens from London. The tube and train station is only a few minutes' walk from the Victoria Gate. The District Line will take you on the tube to Kew Gardens and the overland train (South West Trains) runs from London Waterloo to Kew Bridge Station.

Car – At only 8 miles from central London, Kew Gardens should only take around 30 minutes journey time, depending on traffic. There is a cark park at Kew Gardens (which postcode TW9 3AB will take you to), but it is limited to 300 cars. All day parking costs £7.

River – Certainly not the quickest method, but a pretty one if you have the time. From April until October, Westminster Passenger Services (**www.wpsa.co.uk**) provide a scheduled service from Westminster Pier to Kew (and onwards to Richmond and Hampton Court.) The journey takes 90 minutes to Kew, but this is subject to tides and can change quite significantly.

LEEDS CASTLE

Credit VisitEngland/VisitKent

The 900 year old Leeds Castle is a spectacular, breath taking site, set in 500 acres of beautiful parkland and formal gardens in the heart of Kent.

The moat surrounded castle is a breathtaking vision, open all year round with something to interest and entertain every visitor. Leeds Castle has a wealth of attractions and is one of the most visited historic buildings in Britain.

Attractions

- The Castle – Indulge in the remarkable history of Leeds Castle from the days of the Norman stronghold, medieval queens, King Henry VIII, right through to the current day. An audio tour is available to enrich your experience.

- The Dark Sky Experience – Launching in May 2015 in celebration of the 600th anniversary of Agincourt. The attraction will allow visitors to explore and experience the victory of King Henry V as he defeated a mighty French army at Agincourt in 1415.

- Maze and underground grotto – a unique maze made up of 2,400 yew trees. The underground grotto is on the exit made from shells, minerals and wood.

- Falconry – an impressive Bird of Prey centre with 22 birds on public display. Falconry displays are put on at 2pm daily (April to September) and 1.30pm at weekends (October to March.) Birds include Hawks, Vultures, Owls and Falcons.

- 2 Adventure Playgrounds – The Knights Realm Playground is built entirely of wood and will keep the kids entertained with secret tunnels, slides, rope walkways and towers. For younger children under the age of 6 is Squires' Courtyard Playground with sand pits, slides, swings and climbing on offer.

- The Dog Collar Museum – An unusual museum displaying a unique collection of 100 dog collars spanning five centuries.

- The Gatehouse Exhibition – See original artefacts, illustration and film all explaining the special history of Leeds Castle.,

- The Grounds – Enjoy exploring The Wood Garden, The Culpeper Garden, and The Lady Baillie Mediterranean Garden Terrace.

- 500 acres of parkland

- Other experiences include golf, Segway, Go Ape, Hot Air Balloon Flights and Wildlife Experiences.

- Various events take place throughout the year, please see the website for further details.

Admission

Your ticket allows you entry to Leeds Castle all year. For a 10% discount, book online in advance.

Tickets cost £24 for adults, £16 for children (4-15 years) and £21 concessions.

The grounds of Leeds Castle open 10am daily. The Castle is open from 10.30am daily with the last admission from April to September at 4.30pm and the gates closing at 6pm.

During October to March the last admission is 3pm with the gates closing at 5pm.

Please note the castle is closed during firework weekend in November and on Christmas Day.

Money Saving Tip 1 – If you travel by train to Leeds Castle you can take advantage of the 2 for 1 entry. To claim your offer please download your voucher here **www.visitkentoffers.co.uk**

www.leeds-castle.com – 01622 880008 – Leeds Castle, Maidstone, Kent, ME17 1PL

Getting There From London

Car – Located 45 miles from central London with an approximate drive time of 1 hour and 15 minutes via the A2. Leeds Castle is near Maidstone in Kent, at Junction 8 of the M20 between London and the Channel Ports. A free car park is available at Leeds Castle.

Train – Direct trains go from London Victoria to Bearsted Station, taking just over 1 hour. There is a coach shuttle service available from **www.spottravel.co.uk** from April to September. A private service is available from October until March. Please see the Spot Travel website for prices and times.

THE NEW FOREST

VisitEngland/New Forest District Council

The New Forest officially became a National Park in 2005. The unspoiled ancient woodland and wide open heathland is dotted with beautiful, picturesque towns and villages, stretching across south-west Hampshire, south-east Wiltshire and towards east Dorset.

If you head away from the towns, villages and car parks, you can easily find yourself in the peace and tranquility of the forest, blow away the cobwebs and appreciate the rewards of nature away from modern day living. Due to the vastness of the area you can easily find spots that allow you to imagine you are the only one there.

Ponies, donkeys, cattle and pigs roam freely throughout the forest, adding to the wild and natural feel of the park. The ponies are greater in number so you are more likely to spot one of these. Although they are friendly (being used to visitors), I would recommend admiring them from a short distance away, not only for safety reasons, but also to not frighten them. Please do not be tempted to feed them, it is forbidden and can incur a fine.

A day trip to the New Forest from London will offer you a taster of what a longer trip could offer. Although perfectly accessible from London for the day, the sheer size and number of experiences available would require a stay of at least a few days, more likely a week, to fully appreciate.

But that's not to say you can't have a very special day out. Arrive early (the first train from London arrives in Brockenhurst at 7.17am) and use this guide to plan out what you want to see to make the most of your day.

Money Saving Tip – For £5 you can buy a discount card giving you access to various offers in the New Forest. Available from businesses supporting the scheme or from the visitor centre in Lyndhurst. **www.brandnewforest.com**

History of the New Forest

The New Forest, despite its name, has a long and unique history, existing as a woodland since the end of the last Ice Age. The New Forest was created as a royal forest and hunting ground in 1079 by William the Conqueror. The fascinating history of the New Forest continued through Tudor times, the period when Henry VIII broke with Rome to establish the Church of England. A full insight to the fascinating history of The New Forest can be found here **www.newforestnpa.gov.uk**

Places To See In the New Forest

As mentioned before, there really is so much to see and do in the New Forest, you will be spoilt for choice. There are museums, farms, award winning gardens, historic houses, shopping, horse riding, wildlife parks, cycling, beaches and of course just enjoying the wild nature and freedom of the area.

Main Towns and Villages

Brockenhurst

If you are catching the train from London Waterloo, you will arrive in Brockenhurst. It is one of the largest villages in the New Forest where ponies and donkeys can be seen in the high street. Brockenhurst is a delightful village with restaurants, cafes and high quality shops. The open forest and woodland walks can be easily accessed from Brockenhurst, making it the perfect starting point for your day in the New Forest. Why not hire a bike and explore the surrounding area on wheels?

Lyndhurst

The town of Lyndhurst is another main hub of the New Forest, and is the 'capital' of the forest. It is a sizable town with lots of tea rooms, fine restaurants, pubs and shops. It is also home to Visitor Centre with helpful staff on hand to advise you on all matters relating to the forest.

Within Lyndhurst, visit the church of St Michael and All Angels where the grave of former Lyndhurst resident Alice Liddell can be seen (the inspiration for Lewis Carroll's Alice in Wonderland.)

Learn about the history and heritage of the forest with a visit to the New Forest Museum.

Lymington

The charming waterside market town of Lymington is a beautiful town to explore. A well-known yachting town with a marina and cobbled quay. There is a wide choice of dining options and a great selection of high quality and unique shops.

The pretty Georgian High Street puts on a traditional street market each Saturday, first established in 1250. Market stalls sell food produce, antiques, craft items, plants, bric-a-brac and other general market items. The market runs from 8am until 16.00.

If you fancy getting on the water, take a boat trip around the Solent from Lymington Marina. Puffin Cruises (**www.puffincruiseslymington.com**) offer half hour river cruises, a 1 hour picnic cruise, a 1.5 hour 3 Forts cruise (taking in Henry VII's Hurst Castle, Fort Albert and Fort Victoria), or a Needles Rocks and Lighthouse cruise. Please check the website for prices and departure days/times.

Lymington is also home to St Barbe Museum and Art Gallery, **www.stbarbe-museum.org.uk** a family friendly museum with lots of interactive opportunities for children.

Sway

Not far from Lymington is the small village of Sway, on the edge of the New Forest. Although small, Sway is a bustling village with a railway station, places to eat and an award winning butchers. Sway is also well known for its 220ft 17th century tower, now a listed building.

Burley

Burley is a unique village that time forgot. Burley is another place where ponies and cattle can be found around the streets of the village. Thatched cottages, gift shops, tea rooms and nearby heathland for walking or cycling, make Burley the perfect place for relaxing and enjoying the old world charm of the village.

Burley is known for witchcraft, smuggling and dragons, adding to the village's unique allure. In the 1950's a famous 'white' witch called Sybil Leek once lived in Burley, walking around the village in a long black cloak and her pet jackdaw on her shoulder. Many Burley gift shops sell cauldrons, broomsticks and other witchcraft items! Head for the famous 'A Coven of Witches,' named by the famous witch, and stocking a variety of giftware.

Burley has its very own cider farm. Head for the post office and look for the cider barrel, follow the directions from here to New Forest Cider **www.newforestcider.co.uk**. Enjoy sampling some of the traditionally brewed cider with English apples from their own orchard, together with Cider fruit from Herefordshire and Somerset.

Beaulieu

VisitEngland/Paul Close

The picture postcard perfect village of Beaulieu dates back to the 13th century and is a great location for visitors to explore. With a range of shops including arts, crafts, chocolate, village stores and gift shops.

The world famous Bealieu National Motor Museum was founded by the current Lord Montagu of Bealieu. The museum has many iconic cars from all over the world. Your entry ticket includes the following;

National Motor Museum

With over 250 motor vehicles, showcasing the first motor carriages in Britain up to the present day. Also on display are F1 racers and famous cars from TV and film, including Harry Potter, James Bond, Mr. Bean, Only Fools and Horses, Wallace and Gromit and Heartbeat. Currently there is a Top Gear Exhibition, displaying many of the cars used in the well-known Top Gear Challenges! Your entry ticket also includes the following highlights;

Palace House – a Victorian gothic styled country home.

Beaulieu Abbey – Visit the conserved ruins of what was once a large medieval abbey.

Secret Army Exhibition – Learn about the Secret Operations Executive agents from World War II.

Gardens – Explore the glorious grounds and immaculate lawns of the Palace House.

Monorail and Veteran Bus – Ride the monorail around the grounds or take a ride on the replica 1912 veteran open top bus.

Milford-on-Sea

The charming and traditional village of Milford-on-Sea has some fantastic cliff top walks and a long shingle beach. The village has numerous eateries, including pubs, restaurants and cafes, alongside the usual high street shops.

Head to Sturt Pond for a spot of crabbing from the bridge, or spot the villages very own Forest Ponies grazing by the pond.

Nearby is Hurst Castle www.hurstcastle.co.uk, built by King Henry VIII as a coastal fortress. Catch a ferry from Keyhaven Harbour, or walk along the 1.5 mile shingle spit from Milford-on-Sea. Hurst Castle is open from April until September. Please visit the English Heritage site www.english-heritage.org.uk for opening times and latest prices.

For more things to do in Milford-on-Sea please visit the **www.Milfordonsea.org** website

Exbury Gardens & Steam Railway
200 acres of beautifully captivating gardens. The steam train can take you on a 1 and a quarter mile loop through the gardens, allowing you to sit back and relax and enjoy the stunning scenery going past.

The gardens are a brilliant mix of formal and natural and depending on the time of year, you will be treated to a colourful display of rhododendrons, camellias, magnolias and azaleas among other beautiful flowers. For full detail of all the displays at Exbury Gardens, please visit their website. www.exbury.co.uk

There are 3 wood and parkland areas that kids will love to explore. Keep an eye out for a range of birds, pheasant, squirrels, dragonflies and butterflies in the summer. Children will have fun looking for plants that existed before and during the time of the dinosaurs! There is an adventure playground area

Pack a picnic and enjoy it in one of the two designated picnic areas.

Exbury is open from March until November, 10am until 4.30pm. Admission prices start at £11 for adults (off peak) – please see the website for a full price list.

Lepe Country Park
Lepe Country Park is the perfect place to enjoy the coast with over a mile of beach and incredible views over the Solent. Historic D-Day remains can be seen along the beach, where thousands of troops left Britain for the Normandy beaches.

Families will love Lepe Country Park with an adventure playground, waterfront walks, birdwatching and picnic spots.

For more information visit **www3.hants.gov.uk**

Getting Around the New Forest
There are a variety of ways to get around The New Forest with ease.

Bike

Hire a bike and explore the area on wheels. With over 100 miles of cycle routes within the forest, much of it off road and traffic free, it provides a brilliant way for everyone, including children, to get around. If you arrive by train, you can hire a bike at the station from www.countrylanes.co.uk or **www.newforestcyclehire.co.uk**

Tour

An open top bus experience is a fantastic way to explore the forest, taking you through historic villages, open countryside and the stunning coastline. Tours run daily from late June to mid-September. There is a choice of 3 routes. You can switch between routes and hop on and off along the way. You can use your ticket for discounts in local restaurants, pubs and attractions.

Red Route – Lyndhurst, Burley, Ringwood, Fordingbridge, Sandy Balls, Ashurst, New Forest Wildlife Park, Lyndhurst. This route takes in northern part of the New Forest.

Green Route – Lyndhurst, Brockenhurst, Lymington, Beaulieu, Exbury Gardens, Hythe Ferry, Lyndhurst

This route takes in the south east of the New Forest.

Blue Route – Lymington, Brockenhurst, Burley, New Milton, Barton-On-Sea, Milford-On-Sea, Keyhaven, Lymington

This route takes in the south west of the New Forest, the coast and the beach.

During the school summer holidays the Beach Bus runs until 1st September, linking Lymington with Hythe, with stops including Bucklers Head, Exbury Gardens and Lepe Country Park. The service runs hourly, 7 days a week.

For further information and ticket prices please see the New Forest Tour website. **www.thenewforesttour.info**

Bus

Local buses run year round. Bluestar has 3 bus routes, the number 6 being the best option, linking Lymington, Brockenhurst, Lyndhurst and Ashurst. More Wilts & Dorset is another local bus company with services linking Lymington, Everton and New Milton with Bournemouth.

Car

You can drive around the forest to reach various towns, villages and walking spots. Car parks are found throughout. If you are driving within the forest please remember to drive slowly and be very aware of the free roaming animals. Towns and villages can get congested, especially during summer months.

In the Area

As the New Forest is a huge area, I won't list nearby attractions, there isn't really much time for any detours. If you did decide to stay for longer, there are the beautiful sandy beaches of Bournemouth and Poole not far away. The very picturesque quayside town of Christchurch to the south of the New Forest is also a great place to explore.

This is not a complete guide to the New Forest. It should be used as an introduction to give you some ideas on where you might like to visit on a day trip from London. I think the New Forest is a magical place that offers endless opportunities for days out. I hope you love it as much as I do!

Getting There From London

The New Forest National Park, Lyndhurst, SO43 7NY (for the Visitor Centre)

By Car – Lyndhurst in The New Forest is approximately 90 miles from central London, so, depending on traffic, about 2 hours.

By Train – Direct trains go from London Waterloo to Brockenhurst in The New Forest. They take 1 hour and 40 minutes.

Further Information

Lyndhurst Visitor Information Centre, Main Car Park, Lyndhurst SO43 7NY

www.thenewforest.co.uk – info@thenewforest.co.uk – 023 8028 2269

OXFORD

Photo Credit: VisitEngland/VisitOxfordshire

Oxford is one of the world's most famous university towns. Oxford University is the oldest university in Britain, dating back to the 13th century. Although the Oxford is known for its famous university, it offers more. Oxford does a great job in combining the rich history and culture of the city with the more modern day attractions.

Oxford has plenty of green spaces and parks to relax in, alongside museums and galleries. The centre is compact enough that getting around on foot is not a problem.

Harry Potter fans will love Oxford. The filming of Hogwarts School took place in a number of locations, 2 of which are in Oxford; The Great Hall of Christ Church College and Bodleian Library. Bodleian Library at Oxford University was also where Oscar Wilde, C S Lewis and J R R Tolkien once studied.

University Church of St. Mary the Virgin

The Church of St Mary the Virgin is the University's own church, providing fantastic panoramic views of the city. Out of the towers you can climb in Oxford, it probably provides the best views, so if you can only climb one, pick this one.

The tower dates back to 1280 with 127 steps leading you up to the top, past the Clore Old Library and the historic bell ringing chamber.
Entry to the church is free but there is a charge (£4) to go up the tower. The stone stairs are quite narrow and get very steep, there is an iron rail to hold on to.

The tower is open every day from 9am until 6pm Monday to Saturday, 11.30am until 6pm on Sundays (July & August) with slightly shorter opening times for the rest of the year.
www.university-church.ox.ac.uk – High Street, Oxford, OX1 4BJ

Christ Church College

Photo Credit: VisitEngland/VisitOxfordshire

One of the biggest and most famous colleges of the University of Oxford. Christ Church College is breathtakingly beautiful.

There is the world famous choir, two famous landmarks (Tom Tower and the Cathedral spire) and the peaceful Christ Church Meadow, with cattle happily grazing!

Of course, aside from being an internationally acclaimed university, that has seen many well-known names, it is also now the place where parts of Harry Potter was filmed! It was of course also the inspiration for Lewis Carroll to write all about Alice in Wonderland.

A great way to gain an insight into the fascinating history of Christ Church College, including scenes from the Harry Potter films and the places Lewis Carroll was inspired by, is by a guided tour. Tours last about an hour and are led by knowledgeable and experienced Christ Church custodians.

Tour Prices cost £13 per adult and £11 for children and concessions.

The Cathedral welcomes visitors with free guided tours available on weekdays at 11am, 12 noon, 2pm and 3pm, lasting 20 minutes. Learn about the history, architecture and life of the cathedral. If you have time, attend a service and listen to the choir sing. Check the website for service times.

Admission
Do check the website ahead of time to confirm what is open when. Entry costs from July to August are £9 for adults, children (5-17) and concessions is £8. A family ticket is £18. Discounts are given when the cathedral or hall are closed.

Pssst...
You can spend the night at Christ Church College and eat breakfast in The Great Hall! Take a look here for availability and prices **www.universityrooms.com**

www.chch.ox.ac.uk – Christ Church College, St Aldate's, Oxford, OX1 1DP

Bodleian Library
One of the oldest and greatest public libraries in the world with millions of items resting on miles of shelves. The library dates back to 1602, when it was first opened to scholars.

Bodleian Library is a must see, a working library which forms part of the University of Oxford. If your itinerary allows, I would recommend going on a Sunday as the reading areas are accessible then.

The history of the library is incredible. The 1 hour long tours are worthwhile to fully understand the history.

The reading rooms have witnessed generations of famous students including Oscar Wilde, CS Lewis, JRR Tolkien, 26 prime ministers, 5 kings and 40 Nobel Prize winners.

Tours
It is well worth taking a guided tour to learn more about the history and heart of the library. Explore the Divinity School, see where Parliament was held in the Civil War and look inside the Chancellor's Court room. You will also visit Duke Humfrey's medieval library which has been home to many famous scholars in the past.

Tours cost £7 per person (only suitable for children over the age of 11.) Certain tours can be booked in advance via this website, **www.bodleian.ox.ac.uk**
The Weston Wing is home to some fantastic exhibitions. The latest one 'Marks of Genius'(on until 20th September 2015) highlights some incredible items including the dust jacket from 'The Hobbit,' the

handwritten 'Wind in the Willows,' Shakespeare's 'The First Folio,' pages from the draft of 'Frankenstein' and other remarkable maps, manuscripts and books.

Divinity School

Originally built in 1488 for the teaching of theology, the Divinity School is an incredible example of English Gothic architecture. This room was the first examination hall.

The cost of entry is £1 per person which children under 5 going free. It is open Monday to Friday from 9am until 5pm, Saturday 9am until 4.30pm and Sunday 11am until 5pm.

Opening Times: 7 days a week, apart from Christmas and Easter. Most days it opens at around 9am and closes at 5pm but this does vary so please check on the website.

www.bodleian.ox.ac.uk – Broad Street, Oxford OX1 3BG, England – +44 1865 287400

Museums

Pitts Rivers Museum

With items from throughout human history from all over the world, the Pitt Rivers Museum has one of the best collection of anthropology and archaeology.

Admission is free. The museum is open every day apart from Mondays (open on Bank Holiday Mondays.) **www.prm.ox.ac.uk**

Ashmolean Museum of Art and Archaeology

This museum is the oldest in the UK and one of the oldest in the world, dating back to 1683. The museum is home to the University's large collections of antiques and arts.

The museum has a major collection on anthropological displays and makes for a very interesting visit. There is an excellent variety of art and culture from around the world from ancient time's right up to the present day.

The museum is located on Beaumont Street and is open every day apart from Mondays (except Bank Holiday Mondays.) The opening hours are 10am until 5pm. Admission is free.
www.ashmolean.org

University Museum of Natural History

Another free to enter museum – the University of Natural History holds 4.5 million specimens and is the one of the largest collections of its type.

The museum is open from 10am until 5pm daily.
www.oum.ox.ac.uk

Magdalen College

One of the most prominent and beautiful of the colleges in Oxford. Set in 40 hectares of river walks and large green lawns. All in the centre of the city. If you can, make this a priority to see in Oxford, you won't regret it.

Magdalen College is a busy college but visitors are welcome at regular times of the day. The main areas of the college that are usually open are the Hall, Chapel and Old Kitchen Bar. You can also enjoy the surrounding grounds, parkland and gardens, with walks along the River Cherwell and views of the Deer Park. This is a great spot to have a picnic on a pleasant day, with river boats and punts going by.

Double check on the website before visiting, but current opening times are 12 noon until 7pm (June – September) and 1pm until 6pm or dusk (rest of the year.) Entry costs £5 for adults, £4 concessions, family ticket £14 (children under 7 are free.)

www.magd.ox.ac.uk

University of Oxford Botanic Garden
The oldest Botanic garden in Britain. Handily located in the city centre it is the perfect place to relax and enjoy the uniquely diverse collection of plants. With 5,000 different plant species growing, both outside in 2 main gardens and within a selection of 7 different glasshouses. Families are welcome with activity trails and activities on offer for children.

Entry is £4.95 per adult, concessionary is £3.30 and children are free.
www.botanic-garden.ox.ac.uk – The University of Oxford Botanic Garden, Rose Lane, Oxford OX1 4AZ

Radcliffe Camera

VisitEngland/Experience

A classic Oxford landmark and one of the city's most photographed buildings. Radcliffe Camera was built between 1737 and 1749, designed to house a library. There is no public access to the building, it now contains two reading rooms, mainly used by undergraduates.

The Covered Market
Head to the Covered Market in Oxford for a variety of shops (clothes, jewellery, electronics etc.), cafes, butchers and fruit and vegetable stalls. The market is open 7 days a week from 8am until 5.30pm Monday to Saturday and 10am until 4pm on Sundays.
www.oxford-coveredmarket.co.uk – Market St. Oxford OX1 3DZ

A Punt down The River

VisitEngland/Experience Oxfordshire

The quintessential Oxford experience. A visit to Oxford wouldn't be complete without a punt down one of the famous rivers. Choose from Cherwell River or the Thames.

For Cherwell, visit Cherwell Boathouse **www.cherwellboathouse.co.uk** to hire a punt either by the hour (£15 weekdays, £18 weekends) or for a full day (£75 week days, £90 weekends.)

For a punt on the River Thames head to Salter's Steamers **www.salterssteamers.co.uk** where you can hire a punt for £20 an hour or £60 for 4 hours or £100 for a full day (8 hours.) If you want to chill out a bit, you can hire a 'chauffeur' for your punt for £60 an hour.

Oxford Tours

A great way to get a feel for a place and a lot of knowledgeable information, is to take a tour. Here are a selection that may interest you;

Oxford City Sightseeing Tours – They run all year round (apart from 25th/26th December and 1st Jan), and are available as either 24 hour or 48 hour tickets. They are perfect if you are catching the train up to Oxford from London as it will enable you to get on at the first stop, just outside the train station. Other stops include Bodleian Library, Christ Church College, Carfax Tower, Alice's Shop and many more Oxford highlights. Adult 24 hour tickets cost £14, Child tickets £7, Students £12, Seniors £10 and Family £37. Please visit their website for full details and booking **www.city-sightseeing.com**

Oxford Official Guided Walking Tours – All tours leave from the Oxford Visitor Information Centre. There are a wide range of tour choices, both public and private. Choices include Literary Tour, Medieval Tour, Oxford Films Site Tour, Stained Glass Tour, Science at Oxford Tour, Tudor Oxford Tour and many more. The most popular tour is the University and City Tour (sometimes including Divinity School) which is an introductory tour to the city, revealing the rich history of Oxford City and the University. Please visit this site for full details and prices **www.visitoxfordandoxfordshire.com**

Eat and Drink

The Old Bookbinders Ale House – A short walk from the city centre is this family run pub serving quality food in a traditional pub atmosphere. Closed on Mondays.
www.oldbookbinders.co.uk – 17-18 Victor Street, Jericho, Oxford, OX2 6BT – 01865 553549

The White Rabbit – A lovely and welcoming pub in central Oxford serving very reasonably priced and delicious pizzas.
www.whiterabbitpizza.co.uk – 21 Friars Entry, Oxford, OX1 2BY – 01865 241177

Vaults & Garden Cafe – Set in a unique building, the Vaults & Garden serves tasty, fresh and seasonal breakfast, lunch and afternoon tea.
www.thevaultsandgarden.com – University Church, High Street, Oxford, OX1 4AH – 01865 279112

Visitor Information Centre

www.visitoxfordandoxfordshire.com – **Info@visitoxfordshire.org** – 15-16 Broad Street, Oxford, OX1 3AS - Telephone: 01865 252200

In the Area

In my opinion, Oxford undoubtedly offers more than enough to fill a whole day. However, should you find yourself in the area again, the following are not far away.

Blenheim Palace

Photo Credit – VisitEngland/Blenheim Palace/Pete Seaward

The birthplace of Sir Winston Churchill and home to the 12th Duke and Duchess of Marlborough. Blenheim Palace is a World Heritage Site set in over 2,000 acres of formal gardens and parkland. There is a lot to see and do at Blenheim Palace so you might want to allow enough time to see it all. It really deserves another day trip all by itself. If you only have a limited time then have a look at the suggested itineraries on the website. **www.blenheimpalace.com**

Entry prices start at £13.50 for an adult ticket to access the park and gardens. To also enter the Palace (and park and gardens), adult tickets cost £22.50.

Blenheim Palace is 10 miles north of Oxford on the A34. If you are without a car it is possible by bus. The S3 bus service to Woodstock runs every 30 minutes from Oxford train station to the gates of Blenheim Palace. You can even buy your tickets for the palace on the bus to receive a discount to the palace. The journey takes about 40 minutes by bus. **www.stagecoachbus.com**

Bampton Village

VisitEngland/VisitOxfordshire

19 miles away is the pretty small Cotswold Village of Bampton. A must see for any Downton Abbey fans. Take a walk around the village and see Mrs. Crawley's house, the church, the entrance to the hospital and where the memorial was built in the fifth season. Tours of the village are available for £7.50 (adults) £3.50 (child) and £7 concessions.

Please book here **www.visitoxfordandoxfordshire.com**

Getting There From London
Train – Direct trains leave from London Paddington arriving in Oxford in under 1 hour.

Car – Oxford is just under 60 miles from London via the M40 and A40. Journey time should be about 1 hour 20 minutes. The best option is to use one of the Park and Ride car parks to get into the city centre **www.oxfordshire.gov.uk**

PARIS

Paris hardly requires an introduction. Known the world over as one of the most beautifully captivating capitals to immerse yourself in, it is a city brimming with sophistication and cultural treasures. Paris is strewn with shops oozing Parisian style and unique street side cafes serving up deliciously tempting pastries, cafe noir or other culinary delights. The iconic buildings, museums, galleries and gardens are dotted throughout the relatively compact centre, with the majestic Seine running through.

Perhaps to suggest Paris as a day trip would surprise some people, it is after all a destination that demands a much longer stay to do the city justice. A day trip will only scratch the surface of the incredible delights to be unraveled. I offer Paris as a day trip option as a mere introduction. A snap shot and overview to tempt you to come back for more. Paris deserves it.

As long as you know this, and are motivated enough with a game plan, Paris can be done.
With the opening of the channel tunnel in 1994, you can leave London on the Eurostar train as early as 5.40am and be in Paris for breakfast by 9.30am (further Eurostar details can be found under the 'Getting There' section at the end of this chapter.)

I will discuss in further detail the option of an organised tour versus a do it yourself option. But for now, let's have a run through of the highlights and gems of this richly intriguing city.

The Eiffel Tower

Without a doubt, virtually every visitor to Paris has this on their itinerary. As one of the most recognised and iconic landmarks in the world, seeing it in real life is an entry on most people's bucket lists. The Eiffel Tower opened in 1889 having taken over 2 years to build. The construction time comes as small surprise given the 18,000 metal parts and 2.5 million rivets that were used to build the 324 metre high tower.

Weighing in at a hefty 10,100 tonnes the tower was named after Gustave Eiffel, the engineer's company who designed and constructed it.

The Eiffel Tower (or La tour Eiffel in French) was erected as the entrance arch to the 1889 World's Fair. It is the most visited paid monument in the world, with 2010 seeing its 250 millionth visitor!
It is possible to climb the 1,665 steps to get to the second level (where an elevator is the only way to get to the viewing platform at 276m high.) If you are not feeling energetic, fear not, you can take a lift from the bottom. On a clear day you can see some spectacular views reaching out as far as 80km. If you are a little weary of heights, it might be of some comfort to know that the viewing platform is within an iron cage.

TIP: Buy your tickets online in advance to avoid the colossal queues on the day.

Admission – Adult prices to get to the top currently cost 15.5€ and children between the ages of 4 and 11 costs 11€. Please check the website for other prices.
Opening – The Eiffel Tower is open every day of the year from 9am to midnight from mid-June to early September and from 9.30am to 11pm throughout the rest of the year.

TIP: Make the most out of your visit with the hour long official visitor guide downloaded as an app to your device (doesn't require WIFI after download.) Aside from the audio commentary visitors can use the HD 360° panorama to easily navigate the surrounding landscape and find your way around the monument. The cost to download is 2.99€. **www.toureiffel.paris**

Louvre Museum
This historic landmark, the most visited museum in the world, first opened in 1793 with 537 paintings. Fast forward to the present day, and there are now over 35,000 works of art.
The Louvre is enormous. You couldn't possibly attempt to cover even a small section of it in just one visit, squeezed into a day trip. But don't let this put you off, with a little forward planning you can, and should, at least attempt to set foot inside. Do your research before you go, be familiar with the layout via their website, and prioritize what you want to see.

Of course, the Louvre is known the world over for Leonardo da Vinci's Mona Lisa painting which can be found on the 1st floor of the museum.

Museum Tours
I encourage you to check out the various tour options in advance of your visit to the Louvre. Like the Eiffel Tower, you can purchase an official app for around €1.79 which can be used on an iPhone or Android device. One of the options within the app is the 'Masterpieces Tour' which will incorporate the Mona Lisa amongst other famous highlights. **www.louvre.fr**

Alternatively, you can go on a guided tour with a National Museum Guide. These tours also cover the 'Louvre's Masterpieces' and last an hour and a half. They can however only be bought on the day of your visit. Details of all of these options can be found on the official Louvre website.

TIP: To save time on the day, tickets can be purchased in advance via links on the official website.

Admission – Prices start at €12 for entry to the permanent collections (on the first Sunday of the month from October to March, entry is free, please confirm on the official website for exceptions.)

Opening – The Louvre is open from 9am until 6pm every day (except Tuesday.) On Wednesday and Friday nights the museum is open until 9.45pm. The Louvre is closed on Christmas Day, New Year's Day and May 1st.

Address – Musée du Louvre, 75058 Paris – France - +33 (0)1 40 20 53 17 or **www.louvre.fr**
Nearest Métro: Palais-Royal Musée du Louvre (lines 1 and 7)

Other Highlights

As you know, Paris warrants a guide book all of its own. I couldn't possibly attempt to cover everything to see and do in one chapter. Listed below are other highlights of Paris and is by no means conclusive;

Musee d'Orsay – Housed in a former train station, this world class museum with a huge collection of French Impressionist artwork.

Notre Dame Cathedral – Enchanting, beautiful, breathtaking. One of my favourite Paris landmarks. A stunning gothic cathedral that you at least have to see the outside of. You are unlikely to have the time to queue to climb the tower, but it is amazing. 420 steps to the top, on a clear day the views are outstanding.

Palais Garnier, Opera National de Paris – A stunning building, the inspiration for The Phantom of the Opera. With rooms beyond your imagination, with gold and marble, sculptures, paintings, chandeliers. The magnificence of this place, dedicated to opera and ballet, will take your breath away.

River Seine – Walk along the beautiful banks of the River Seine, now a UNESCO World Heritage Site, or take a boat cruise and take in some iconic Paris landmarks.

Arc de Triomphe – One of the most famous landmarks in Paris, the Arc de Triomphe is located at the western end of the Champs-Élysées. The arch was built between 1806 and 1836 in honour of the soldiers who fought in the Napoleonic Wars. You can enjoy the Arc de Triomphe from ground level from the Champs-Élysées, or climb the 40 steps to the top (€9.50 adults, €6 concessions, Under 18's free.) **www.arc-de-triomphe.monuments-nationaux.fr/en/**
Sacre Coeur – The design and craftmanship of this church is incredible, both inside and outside. Marvel at the mosaics on the inside and admire the views from the top of the hill. Open every day from 6.30am until 10.30pm. Entry is free. **www.sacre-coeur-montmartre.com**

Tours in Paris

What I would really recommend to do is take an organised tour, whether it is a walking tour or a bus tour. This way you can get to places quickly and under the guidance of an experienced tour guide.
These are tours you can take when you arrive in Paris, rather than the ones that escort you from London.

L'Open Tour Paris

One way to squeeze lots of sights into one day would be to take a bus tour. L'Open Tour is a particularly good one as they have a stop right outside Gare du Nord (where your Eurostar will be coming in to.)
With buses leaving every 10 minutes you won't be wasting time hanging around. There are an incredible amount of stops across their 4 different routes, there are 50 stops in total!

There are audio guides to listen to in a variety of languages, as you travel between stops.

The 4 routes are as follows;

Paris Grand Tour (green line), journey time of 2 hours.
Montparnasse Saint-Germain (orange line), journey time of 1 hour. Montmartre – Grands Boulevards (yellow line), journey time of 1 hour and 20 minutes. Bastille – Bercy (blue line), journey time of 1 hour. It is the Yellow line that has the closest stop to Gare du Nord, stop number 53 on 10 boulevard de Denain.

Admission – Adult tickets cost €32, Child (4-11) €16

Booking – Book online here **www.pariscityvision.com**

Big Bus Tours

Another hop on hop off tour is the Big Bus tour. Buses run every 15 minutes so once you have seen an attraction, you won't have to wait too long for the bus to take you to your next stop. A full circuit takes 2 hours and 20 minutes. You can get on the bus at any one of the stops. Take a look at the map to decide which one is most suitable for you. **www.eng.bigbustours.com**

Tours start at 10am and finish at 8.30pm.

There are 10 stops on the route where you can see the following attractions;
Eiffel Tower, The Arc de Triomphe, Notre Dame, L'Hôtel des Invalides, Palais Garnier, Grand Palais, Louvre and Tuileres Gardens, Place de la Concorde, La Madeleine, Trocadéro, Place Vendôme.

Admission – Adult €30.00 (€27 online), Child (4-12) €16 (€14.40 online.) If you would like to include a boat cruise along the River Seine add another €9 to the adult tickets and €6 to the child tickets.
Booking – If you know you are going to do this trip it makes sense to book it online and make some savings. **www.eng.bigbustours.com**

Sandemans Paris Tour

A great way to explore the city in a limited time frame is to take an organised walking tour. Sandemans offer fantastic tours in 18 cities throughout Europe and come highly recommended.

The Paris tour is led by an expert guide who will take you along the banks of the Seine, Notre Dame, to view the Eiffel Tower, Napoléon's Tomb, view the Champs-Elysées and all the other must see places in Paris. Tours tend to last about 2 and a half hours and are run purely on tips. So you pay the guide what you want to at the end.

Tours run every day at 10am, 11am and 1pm, meeting at the fountain on Place St Michel.
Other tours are available, please check their website for details.
www.newparistours.com

Discover Walks

Discover Walks offer a variety of tours of different lengths. You don't need to pay anything in advance for these tours, you just pay what you want to the guide at the end.
www.discoverwalks.com

Other Tours to Look At

www.cityfreetour.com/paris/

Tour Companies from London

There are a number of tour companies who organise day trips from London to Paris. Whether they are suitable for you or not really comes down to personal choice. There are pros and cons to both organised trips and the do it yourself option.

The organised tours can sometimes feel a bit rushed, where you are trying to cram too much into a short space of time. However, the planning and logistics are all taken care of for you, leaving you to enjoy the day. Depending on when you book your trip, an organised tour can sometimes work out cheaper, see further on for my findings on this!

The do it yourself option does allow for more flexibility, but will require more planning.
As I said, it is all down to personal choice!

Take a look at some of the tour companies and see what they are offering. Then decide which option suits you best. Plenty of people enjoy both methods of visiting Paris.

Golden Tours
At the time of writing, Golden Tours run 9 day trips from London to Paris. The most basic one starts at £118 (adult) £113 (child) with a duration of 16 hours. This includes return seats on the Eurostar and a 1 hour cruise on the River Seine. The most expensive day trip is currently £379 and includes premier reserved seats on the Eurostar, Paris walking tour, a 2 course lunch at the Eiffel Tower and entry to the Louvre. You are fully escorted when in Paris.
www.goldentours.com/trips-to-paris

Premium Tours
Premium Tours currently offer 4 different day trips to Paris. The cheapest starts at £149 (adults) and £139 (child.) This tour seems to be return tickets on the Eurostar with someone at St Pancras International to assist you with checking in. The luxury Paris trip is fully escorted and costs £235 (adult) £225 (child) and includes Eurostar tickets, tour of Paris, Champagne lunch on Eiffel Tower, guided tour of the Louvre, fast entry access to level 1 of the Eiffel Tower and a cruise on the River Seine.
www.premiumtours.co.uk

Evan Evans Tours
Currently offer 3 tours to Paris. The cheapest is £144 (adults) and includes return tickets on the Eurostar and a Visite Paris Card (a travel card to use the Metro.) The escorted tours cost £220 (adults) and includes return tickets on the Eurostar, Hop on hop off Paris Sightseeing Bus, entry to level 2 of the Eiffel Tower and a cruise on the River Seine.
www.evanevanstours.com

Getting to Paris from London Train
The only way I would really recommend to get to Paris from London for a day trip is by the Eurostar. All of the above mentioned organised tours will also be via Eurostar.
To get the best deals, you will need to book as far in advance as you can (up to 6 months is allowed.)

Which is more economical, an organised tour or do it yourself?
In the interest of helping you decide which option is better for you, organised versus do it yourself, these are the results of my findings. Please note that these prices and availability were correct at the time of writing this (14th May 2015.)

To make a fair comparison I have taken prices from the same time trains, on the same days. I have used Golden Tours as the organised tour option. With this tour you also get a 1 hour river cruise, although your trip is not escorted.

I have taken 4 dates to illustrate the benefit of booking in advance.

The outward train is the 7.01am from St Pancras International.
The return train is the 8.13pm from Gare du Nord.

Tuesday May 19th – Golden Tours = £118 v Direct with Eurostar = £259
Tuesday June 16th – Golden Tours = £118 v Direct with Eurostar = £135
Tuesday July 14th – Golden Tours = £118 v Direct with Eurostar = £93.50
Tuesday August 11th – Golden Tours = £118 v Direct with Eurostar = £72

Conclusion – Booking by yourself only becomes more economical when done in advance. If you decide at the last minute to go on a day trip from London to Paris then going the organised tour route is by far the most economical option, especially with a river cruise included. However, if you manage to book at least 2 months in advance, it is cheaper to book it directly yourself.

Once again, please do your own research for your exact days and requirements, this is merely an illustration and times and prices are subject to change.

ROCHESTER

Located in Kent, about 30 miles from central London, Rochester is a unique and historic town, once favoured by the Victorian novelist, Charles Dickens, who owned a house not far away. Many places within the City are from Dicken's novels and are now marked with plaques.

The high street contains many unique independent specialty shops alongside plenty of tempting places to eat and drink.

What to see in Rochester

Rochester Cathedral
Rochester Cathedral is England's second oldest cathedral, founded in 604. See the remains of the medieval wall paintings, the stone pilgrim steps and some interesting tombs. It really is a lovely, tranquil and inspirational Cathedral. Don't miss it.

Tours are available at a cost of £4 per person, and must be booked in advance. Audio tours are also available (currently free of charge due to parts of the building being inaccessible.)

Admission – Entry to the Cathedral is free but donations are welcome.

Opening – At the time of writing this guide, the Cathedral was in the middle of building works, so certain parts of the building were inaccessible. Please double check on their website before visiting.
Opening hours are daily from 7.30am until 6pm (5pm on Saturdays.) Tours are available from 10am until 3.30pm (2pm on Saturdays.)

Address – The Cathedral is in the centre of Rochester, about a 10 minute walk from the train station. The address is The Precinct, Rochester, ME1 1SX

Rochester Castle

Just across the road from the Cathedral is Rochester Castle. One of the best preserved keeps and one of the tallest in the country. Although a ruin, it still has its castle walls and dominates the Rochester skyline, alongside Rochester Cathedral. It is an impressive building with the castle walls reaching over 100 feet tall. The castle has a lively past, with three sieges, the one in 1215 by King John partly demolished it.

Now, visitors can see the rebuilt round tower and climb the many steps for fantastic views of the surrounding area. Please note that the steps are steep and care should be taken.
Audio tours are available to hire for £1. It is available in English, French, German and Dutch.

Admission – Adults £6.20, Child (5-15 years) £3.90, Concessions £3.90, Family (2 adults and 3 children) £16.20.

Money Saving Tip 1 – English Heritage annual membership available or an Overseas Visitors Pass. Please see the chapter on Passes & Discounts for further details.

Money Saving Tip 2 – If you are travelling by train you can get 2 for 1 entry into Rochester Castle **http://www.southeasternrailway.co.uk/offers-and-destinations/2for1/kent-2-for-1-offers/2-for-1-entry-to-rochester-castle**

Opening – 1st April until 30th September, open daily between 10am and 6pm (last admission 45 minutes before closing.) 1st October until 24th March 2016, open daily between 10am and 4pm. Closed 24th, 25th, 26th, 28th December and 1st January.
www.english-heritage.org.uk

Rochester Guildhall Museum

Built in 1687, the Rochester Guildhall tells the story of Rochester and the development of Medway. The 17th century building is fantastic to see, with many fascinating displays including;

- The Dickens Discovery Room – learn about the author's life and works here.
- Victorian kitchen and drawing room
- Full size reconstruction of part of a Medway prison hulk –
- The most complete set of 18th century cabinet maker's tools in the world
- A large selection of paintings and prints of the area
- Free quizzes for children

Opening – Open from 10am to 5pm Tuesdays to Sundays
Contact – **guildhall.museum@medway.gov.uk** – 17 High Street Rochester, Medway ME1 1PY
Admission – The museum is free to enter

Tours

Footsteps in Time

Footsteps in time offer a guided walking tour of Rochester, led by characters from Charles Dickens novels. The entertaining tours last for 90 minutes and will bring to life the beautiful buildings and characters from the famous author. Tickets cost £4.20 per person (minimum of 10 people) and are available in English, French and Spanish.

Bookings must be made in advance via **www.footstepsintimerochester.co.uk** or by calling +44 (0) 1634 818 630.

The City of Rochester Society provide free walking tours of Rochester from Good Friday until October, on selected days. The tours start from The Visitors Centre on the High Street in Rochester at 2.15pm every Saturday, Wednesday and Public Holiday. The tours are free of charge, but any donations to the Society are appreciated. **www.city-of-rochester.org.uk**

In the Area

Chatham Dockyards – Not far from Rochester (2.5 miles) are the historic Chatham Dockyards. Once home to the Royal Navy, it closed in 1984 after several hundred years as one of their main locations. The historic part of the dockyards are now a popular visitor attraction and make for an interesting and educational day out.

There is a lot to see at the dockyards and you may well consider it as a whole day out. The site spans an area of 80 acres in total with historic warships, galleries, museums and various events allowing you to immerse yourself in the fascinating history of the area.

Entry costs £19 per adult, £16.50 concessions, £11.50 children and £49.50 for a family ticket. Tickets are valid for 12 months.

There is free parking for visitors.

If you are using public transport from Rochester, the 141 Arriva bus runs from Star Hill in Rochester to the dockyards. **www.thedockyard.co.uk** -The Sail & Colour Loft, The Historic Dockyard, Church Lane, Chatham, Kent ME4 4TE

Dickens World – Transport yourself back to Victorian times with a 90 minute interactive guided tour of life during the times of the great Charles Dickens. Dickens World is located directly opposite Chatham Dockyards.

The attraction is open to the public on Saturdays and Sunday, it is recommended that you call in advance to check availability. There are also occasionally cancellations on midweek tours so you may get the opportunity to go then. Tour tickets costs £7.50 per person. **www.dickensworld.co.uk**

Getting There From London

Car – Rochester is only 30 miles from London and should take about an hour.

Train – Direct trains leave from both London St Pancras (35 minutes) and London Victoria (45 minutes.) The walk from the train station to the Castle and Cathedral is not far and takes you through the centre of the town.

STONEHENGE

Photo Credit – VisitEngland/English Heritage/Iain Lewis

Known the world over, Stonehenge is at the top of most visitors must see attractions. A UNESCO World Heritage Site, the iconic ancient site is both unique and mysterious. Stonehenge makes for the perfect day trip from London and can easily be combined with either Salisbury nearby, or further afield, Bath.

What is Stonehenge?

We still don't really know why Stonehenge was built. But what we do know, is that people have been attracted to the mystical boulders, weighing in at some 40-tonnes, for over 4,500 years. Stonehenge has drawn visitors for spiritual and pagan worship for many years, as well nearly 1 million tourists each year. Looked after by English Heritage, Stonehenge is one of the most well-known prehistoric monuments in the world. It is still the cause of mystery and debate – why was Stonehenge built? Who managed to erect stones weighing in excess of 40 tonnes? Thoughts include an astronomical calendar, a burial ground or a temple to the sun.

Whatever the reason, they are an incredible and awe inspiring site to witness.

What is the Best Way to See Stonehenge?

Lots of people look at Stonehenge from afar, at the perimeter fence, or whilst driving past on the A303. I think this is missing out on the full experience of the intriguing ancient site. In my opinion, the best way to see Stonehenge is either via an organised tour (see below), or go it alone. Sunrise and sunset, if they fit in with your schedule, are perfect times. Please note, advanced booking is required, with entrance to Stonehenge being via a timed slot.

Top Tip – Stonehenge will be noticeably cooler than London, so dress accordingly. As Stonehenge is situated on top of Salisbury Plain (very flat), it is more exposed to the wind, with little shelter to protect you from the elements. My tip would be, no matter how warm you feel in London, is to layer up.

The Visitor Centre
Newly opened in 2014 is the Visitor Centre, 1 mile from Stonehenge. This is where you will show your tickets and begin your visit, with an exhibition in the centre. This is a fantastic way to learn about Stonehenge. It is interactive and hands on too, so perfect for families to learn too. There is a cafe, toilets and a gift shop. Outside the Visitor Centre are the Neolithic Houses, available to explore how people lived 4,500 years ago. Onward access to Stonehenge can be by either a small Stonehenge shuttle bus or you can walk.

Admission
Stonehenge is open every day apart from Christmas Eve and Christmas Day. A free family audio tour of the stones is included with your entrance. To ensure guaranteed entrance you will need to book in advance (unless you are part of a tour.)

Money Saving Tip – If you are a National Trust Member or English Heritage Member, Stonehenge is included in your pass.

Top Tip – If you want to get closer to the stones and gain access to the inner circle (not possible during normal opening hours) then you can request this via a form on the English Heritage website. An extra fee is payable. This is a popular experience so make sure you book far enough in advance.

Please read the information in the following link for restrictions and guidance. **www.english-heritage.org.uk**

Tickets – Adult tickets starts at £14.50, Concessions £13, Children (5-15) £8.70, Family (2 adults, 3 children) £37.70.

Money Saving Tip – English Heritage and National Trust Members receive free entrance. Please see the **passes and discounts** page for details.

Opening Times – These vary according to the time of year so please check the website for full details. They tend to be 9am until 8pm during the summer months.

Organised Tours

The Stonehenge Tour
As mentioned in the **'Getting There'** section below. The Stonehenge Tour is a double decker bus service that operates from Salisbury train station so perfect for those catching the train down from London. The tour is a hop-on-hop-off service with pick-ups in Salisbury city centre and goes to Old Sarum, through the stunning Wiltshire countryside, and onwards to Stonehenge. Different ticket options are available.

Bus Only – Return journey to Stonehenge (entry not included.) Adult £14, Children (5-15) £9, Family (2 adults & 3 children) £40.
Bus, Old Sarum & Stonehenge – Return bus journey, entry to Stonehenge and visit to Old Sarum. Adult £27, Child £17, Family £78
Bus, Old Sarum, Stonehenge & Salisbury Cathedral – The above option plus entry to Salisbury Cathedral. Adult £33, Child £21, Family £95.

Flying Purple Pig

Great value for money private tours with a personal touch. They offer a variety of tour combinations with Stonehenge included in many options. As an example, they offer a pick-up in central London and drive up to 6 people to Woodhenge and then on to Stonehenge. You have to pay the entrance fee into Stonehenge (see below for details.) The tour lasts for 5 hours and costs £325. So if there were 6 of you that is about £54 per person (plus entry to Stonehenge.)

Please see the website for information on all of their tour options. **www.flyingpurplepig.co.uk**

Salisbury and Stonehenge Guided Tours

Offer a good selection of value for money day trips from London which include Stonehenge in the itinerary. There is a choice of 6 tours, one of which is a 'Stonehenge Direct' tour, which takes place in the afternoon and has various pick up and drop off points within London. You travel in a purpose built mini coach which holds a maximum of 16 people.

The current cost for an adult is £44. **www.stonehenge-tours.com**

Premium Tours

They offer a wide variety of quality tours with Stonehenge featuring in many of them. Combine a visit to Stonehenge with many other attractions, including Bath, Windsor Castle, Stratford, and The Cotswolds. One of their bestselling tours is the Windsor Castle, Stonehenge, Lacock and Bath, including lunch in a 14th century pub. This particular tour costs £90 for adults, £80 for children (3-16yrs) and £87 for concessions. The tour offers great value for money and allows you to fit a lot in to your day without the stresses of organising the transport yourself. The following is included in your price;

- Hotel pick up and drop off
- Entrance to Windsor Castle & Stonehenge
- Pub lunch in 14th century pub in Lacock
- Panoramic Tour of Bath
- Luxury coach and professional guide
-

For details of this tour and many others, please see their website **www.premiumtours.co.uk**

Golden Tours

They offer similar tour selections to Premium Tours and it is worth comparing both before you book to see if any are running any special offers. A visit to Stonehenge is combined with many other locations. They also offer a 'Simple Stonehenge' option (as do Premium Tours), where you can go there for the morning or afternoon. The cost at the time of researching this book was £44 for the morning trip and £39.60 for the afternoon one. It includes the following;

The tour duration is 13 hours, leaving at 8.15am and returning to London at approximately 9pm.
Duration of 5 hours
Entry and extended visit to Stonehenge
Multilingual Audio Guide
Return journey in a luxury coach with free WI-FI.
www.goldentours.com

In the Area

Woodhenge – The lesser known (and less busy!) Woodhenge is not far away (5 miles.) It is thought to have been from the same period as Stonehenge and as the name suggests, is made from wood rather than stone. It is free to see and also looked after by English Heritage. **www.english-heritage.org.uk**

Salisbury – the perfect addition to a day trip to Stonehenge. The town of Salisbury is both impressive and interesting, home to the tallest cathedral in England. See the chapter on Salisbury for full details. Please see the **Salisbury** chapter for details.

Avebury – Looked after by the National Trust, Avebury is the largest prehistoric stone circle in the world. It is also a World Heritage Site. The stones partially surround the village of Avebury, with a museum and Avebury Manor also open to visitors. Access to the stones is free, entrance to the museum and manor is charged.

Avebury is 24 miles from Stonehenge (about 40 minutes in the car.)
Avebury Henge, Green Street, Avebury, Wiltshire, SN8 1RE
Please see the NT website for details. **www.nationaltrust.org.uk**

Getting There From London

Train – Direct trains run directly from London Waterloo to Salisbury. Journey time is about 90 minutes. From there, you can catch a tourist bus to Stonehenge. This tour is a hop on hop off bus which can also include Salisbury Cathedral and Old Sarum. **www.thestonehengetour.info**

Tour – Numerous tours go to Stonehenge, many offering multi destination days out from London. Please see details above.

Car – Stonehenge is just under 90 miles from central London, and depending on traffic, should take around 2 hours. There is a free car park (for people with tickets for Stonehenge, if not, you will have to pay.) It is located next to the Visitor Centre. (Postcode for Sat Nav SP4 7DE.)

SALISBURY

Photo Credit – VisitEngland/Visit Wiltshire/Chris Lock

Exploring Salisbury

Salisbury is a special city in the perfect setting. The surrounding countryside of Salisbury is all lush green fields and quintessential English landscapes. Even Salisbury Cathedral is set amongst picture perfect scenery.

Salisbury is well known for the famous cathedral, but there is much more to Salisbury. The city is easy to get around and has much to delight visitors from London. The historic streets are home to a pleasant mix of independent shops offering unique items alongside the more well-known high street names. Every Saturday and Tuesday (apart from the third Tuesday in October), you will find a bustling market.

If you have time, it is worth exploring one of the many museums within Cathedral Close, choose from;

Arundells – the home of former Prime Minister Sir Edward Heath.
Monpesson House – the perfect example of Queen Anne architecture.
The Rifles Military Museum – tells the story of the infantryman from the Seven Years War to the present day.
Salisbury Museum (including the new Wessex Gallery) – with galleries showing the history of Salisbury. Salisbury is also rich in arts, with many events taking place throughout the year, including the world famous Ageas Salisbury International Arts Festival.

Salisbury caters for any dining and drinking requests, with a tempting range of tea and coffee shops, restaurants, cafes, pubs and bars.

Salisbury Cathedral
You cannot miss the tallest church spire in the UK.

One of the four remaining copies of the Magna Carta is on display within the Chapter House at Salisbury Cathedral, having been well preserved over the years, since it was written in 1215. The historic manuscript was issued by King John of England and stated that everybody, including the King, was subject to the law. If you manage to visit in 2015 you are in for a treat. This year marks the 800th anniversary of the Magna Carta, and so, Salisbury Cathedral will be displaying the legendary piece of history in a new interactive exhibition.

Forgot your watch? Salisbury Cathedral also has the world's oldest working clock on display. Probably the oldest working clock in existence, made of hand-wrought iron in or before 1386.

Salisbury Cathedral is a truly remarkable building, a testimony to the faith and practical skills of the medieval craftsmen who built it but it is much more than a historical monument. It is a living church and a place of prayer. As the Cathedral Church of the Salisbury diocese it is Mother Church of several hundred parishes in Wiltshire and Dorset. It is also a centre of pilgrimage for hundreds of thousands of visitors every year.

Admission

Entry – The suggested voluntary donation is for £7.50 for adults (children within the group free), Students £4.50, Seniors £6.50, Family Tickets (2 adults & 3 children) £15.

Free Tours – Volunteers within the cathedral can take you on a floor tour (no charge) or you can go on a self-guided tour, at your own pace.

Tower Tours – Taking a Tower Tour is the perfect way to get up close to the cathedral's iconic spire. The tour includes a climb of 332 steps via a narrow winding spiral staircase to reach the foot of the spire 225 feet above ground level. You are able to explore the ancient roof spaces whilst learning about the history of the cathedral. The highlight though is stepping out on one of the four balconies and enjoying the stunning views over Salisbury, Old Sarum and the surrounding countryside, the inspiration for John Constable's famous painting 'Salisbury Cathedral from the Water Meadows.'

The tours are led by a Cathedral Guide with 12 spaces available per tour. Due to the popularity of the tours, it is a good idea to book ahead. The cost is £12.50 for adults, £8 for children and £30 for a family ticket (2 adults and 3 children.)

The tours run at least once a day (subject to daily conditions.) Book in advance online here **www.salisburycathedral.digitickets.co.uk**

In the Area

Stonehenge – This is the perfect add on when visiting Salisbury, please see the chapter on **Stonehenge.**

Old Sarum – To the north of the city is the English Heritage site Old Sarum; the location of the original Salisbury Cathedral and castle. **www.english-heritage.org.uk**

Getting There From London

Train – Direct trains run directly from London Waterloo to Salisbury. Journey time is about 90 minutes. You will see the Cathedral when you get off the train, it is about a 10 minute walk from the station.

Car – Salisbury is just under 90 miles via the M3 from London. Journey time should be in the region of 2 hours, traffic dependent.

SANDRINGHAM

Sandringham House is a Grade II listed building located near the village of Sandringham in Norfolk. The country house, set in 20,000 acres of land, has been the private home of British monarchs since 1862.

Her Majesty The Queen enjoys visiting the country retreat, as do the rest of the Royal Family, especially at Christmas time. Visitors are able to also experience the joy of the estate with visits to the house, museum, garden or the country park.

King Edward VII opened the gardens to the public in 1908, and in 1930, King George V opened the museum. In 1977, during the Silver Jubilee year, Her Majesty The Queen opened the house to the public.

What to See at Sandringham House

The House
With knowledgeable guides in each room you can wander around and learn about Royal life at the charming Sandringham House whilst admiring the magnificent furniture, china, paintings and other items on display. The house has a warm feel about it and you can picture the Royal family spending their Christmas there.

Visitors are able to see the main ground floor rooms, which are often used by members of the Royal Family.

The Museum
A brilliantly laid out museum with a fantastic collection of vehicles on display, including miniature toy cars and a pristine Merryweather fire engine from 1939, photos and other memorabilia.

The Gardens
The stunning gardens are a joy to explore, with ponds, lakes, mature trees and rockeries. There is a parish church within the grounds with memorials to many members and relations of the Royal Family. The Royal Family and the Estate staff regularly use the church as a place of worship.

The parish church of St Mary Magdalene, Sandringham, is a country church of exceptional historic interest, with memorials to many members and relations of the Royal Family from Queen Victoria onwards.   It is used regularly as a place of worship by the Royal Family and Estate staff.

You can visit the church from April until September from 11am until 5pm (4pm in October.) There may be occasions when you cannot visit the church due to additional services taking place.

The Country Park
Around 142 hectares of The Queen's private Estate at Sandringham was turned into a country park in 1968. The area was then extended to include more parkland and now stands at 243 hectares.

The park is free to visit and also has free parking available. With lots of woodland paths and walks to discover, it is a brilliant place to explore.

Recommended Time
Allow about 4 hours to visit Sandringham House, Museum & Gardens.

Admission

House, Museum & Gardens – Adult £13.50, Concessions £11.50, Child (5-15) £6.50, Family (2 adults & 3 children) £33.50

Museum & Gardens Only – Adult £9, Concessions £8, Child (5-15) £4.50, Family £22.50
A guided garden tour is an extra £3.50
www.sandringhamestate.co.uk – Sandringham Estate, Sandringham, Norfolk, PE35 6EN

Opening – Sandringham House is open daily from Saturday 4th April 2015 until Sunday October 18th (except Wednesday 29th July.)

Money Saving Tip – Show your bus or rail ticket when buying your ticket and you will only be charged a Museum & Gardens entry fee for a House, Museum & Gardens ticket.

In the Area

Photo Credit – VisitEngland/Iain Lewis

North Norfolk has a beautiful coastline and is well worth a visit if time allows. Much of it is a designated Area of Outstanding Natural Beauty. The whole area has so much to do and this tiny section will not do it justice, it requires a guide book all of its own.

Hunstanton – The classic seaside resort of Hunstanton is 8 miles away, providing traditional seaside fun. Hunstanton is a unique resort with its striped cliffs and is the only west-facing resort on the East coast. Perfect for an ice cream and spot of rock pooling.

Holkham – Recently named as the best beach in Britain by a poll of leading travel journalists, Holkham is a natural and unspoiled beach managed by Natural England in partnership with the Holkham Estate. With large areas of fine sand and bordering soft dunes, Holkham is an incredibly breathtaking beach.

Bircham Windmill – Just 6 miles away from Sandringham is the delightful Birchman Windmill, one of the few windmills left in working order. Visitors can climb the five floors to the fan stage. There are tearooms here, so perfect for an afternoon cream tea and cake.
Address – Great Bircham, King's Lynn, Norfolk, PE31 6SJ. **www.birchamwindmill.co.uk**

Getting there from London

Car – The distance from central London to the Sandringham Estate is about 110 miles, with a journey time of around 2 hours 20 minutes via the M11. Free parking is available at Sandringham House.

Train – The nearest train station to Sandringham House is Kings Lynn, 6 miles away. The journey time from London Kings Cross to Kings Lynn takes about 1 hour and 40 minutes and is a direct service. The Coast Hopper bus runs regularly from the station to Sandringham. A timetable can be found here **www.coasthopper.co.uk**

Coach – National Express coaches run from London Victoria Coach Station to Kings Lynn, although the journey time is quite long, with the fastest taking 3 hours 40 minutes!

STRATFORD-UPON-AVON

The thriving market town of Stratford-upon-Avon is a world class destination, attracting millions of visitors from all over the world. It is a must see place, made famous for being the birthplace and home of William Shakespeare.

This pretty town, with the River Avon running through it, is lined with historic buildings. There is plenty to do in Stratford-upon-Avon, with five fascinating houses, all linked to Shakespeare and his family. Aside from the Shakespeare draw, there are other fantastic opportunities in the town and area to soak up the quintessential English town, packed with 800 years of history, transporting you back in time.

What to see in Stratford-upon-Avon

Shakespeare Properties

There are five Shakespeare properties in and around the town that have been preserved by the Shakespeare's Birthplace Trust, offering visitors a glimpse into 16th century life in England.

Shakespeare's Birthplace

Photo Credit – VisitEngland/Shakespeare's Birth Trust/Amy Murrell

William Shakespeare was born in this Tudor house, located in the centre of Stratford-Upon-Avon in 1564. Whilst he was living here he married Anne Hathaway and they spent their first 5 years together living in the house.

The house has been well preserved with beautifully maintained surrounding gardens.

Visiting the house is a fascinating experience as you get to immerse yourself into the early life of the great writer. Other famous visitors to the house include Charles Dickens, John Keats, Walter Scott and Thomas Hardy.

You will learn about the life of Shakespeare as well as the history of that period of time. There are friendly and knowledgeable costumed guides on hand to answer and questions you might have.
Shakespeare's Birthplace is a very interactive place where you can see daily showings of Shakespeare's plays by a professional troupe of actors. There is a giant wall book in the garden, showing the timeline of 38 of his plays.

There are some great activities to keep the children interested too with various different events taking place throughout the year. Children can take part in quizzes, trails and other activities.
Shakespeare's Birthplace is located on Henley Street in the town centre. Allow at least 1 hour to spend at the house.

Entry: If you are not using the 'Five House Pass' or 'Shakespeare Houses and Gardens Pass'(see below) entry is via the 'Birthplace Pass' which allows you entry to this house, Hall's Croft, Harvard House and Shakespeare's grave. The cost for an adult ticket is £15.90 for an adult, £9.50 for a child, £14.90 for concessions and £41.50 for families. Tickets allow entry for 12 months.

Opening Times: Shakespeare's Birthplace is open year round. From 9am until 5.30pm in the summer, 9am until 5pm in the autumn, 10am until 4pm in the winter and 9am until 5pm in the spring.

Mary Arden's Farm

Set outside Stratford in rural Wilmcote is the timbered Tudor farmhouse where Mary Arden, Shakespeare's mother, lived. With staff dressed in period costumes from Tudor times, taking you back to Shakespeare's time in a fun yet educational way.

There is a lot to see and do here, especially outside, with falconry displays, Tudor archery lessons, wood carving, ironmongery, goose parade and of course all the animals, some of which you can pet. Visitors will learn all about Tudor times, including food preparation, cooking, mealtimes and Tudor music and dancing.

Mary Arden's Farm really is a brilliant place for all the family, pleasing all ages.
There is a cafe serving a great selection of foods and drinks. I recommend at least 2 hours to fully appreciate Mary Arden's Farm.

Getting There: The house and gardens is located about 3 and a half miles from the centre of town in a village called Wilmcote. There is a free car park on site. The train from Stratford-upon-Avon goes to Wilmcote, taking about 7 minutes. Wilmcote train station is about a 5 minute walk from Mary Arden's Farm. Alternatively, if you have the time, the walk will take you about 1 hour from Stratford-upon-Avon.

Entry: Entry to the house and gardens when not bought as part of the Five House Pass costs £9.50 for adults, £5.50 for children, £8.50 for concessions and £24.50 for a family. Your ticket is valid for 12 months.

Opening Times: Mary Arden's Farm is open from March until November, 10am until 5pm daily.

Anne Hathaway's Cottage and Gardens

Anne Hathaway was Shakespeare's wife and you can visit the cottage where she lived, a short walk away from the centre of Stratford. Inside you will see furniture that actually belonged to Anne Hathaway and her family.

The immaculate gardens are beautiful and really enjoyable to spend some time in.

You can reach Anne Hathaway's House with a pleasant walk from the centre of the town, which should take about 20 minutes. Allow about 1 hour for this house.

Getting There: The cottage and gardens are located about 2 miles from Stratford-upon-Avon. Parking is available at the cottage. The walk from town is quite pleasant and takes about 30 minutes.

Entry: Entry to the cottage and gardens when not bought as part of the 'Five House Pass' costs £9.50 for an adult, £5.50 for a child, £8.50 for concessions and £24.50 for a family ticket. Tickets are valid for 12 months.

Opening Times: Open from 9am until 5pm between 16 March and 1 November. Open 10am until 4pm, 2nd November until March 13th.

Hall's Croft

Hall's Croft is where Shakespeare's eldest daughter, Susanna, lived. She lived there with her husband, Dr John Hall. The house has a luxurious appearance with beautiful 16th and 17th century paintings and furnishings.

Guided tours of the house are available to see the 16th and 17th century paintings and furnishings. There is an exhibition on the medicine of that time.

There is a glorious walled garden to explore. Check out the sun dial with the inscription from A Midsummer Night's Dream. There is a herb garden, used back in the day for various 17th century remedies.

Getting There: Located on Old Town, a 5/10 minute walk from Shakespeare's birthplace.

Entry: Hall's Croft is part of both the 'Five House Pass' and the 'Birthplace Pass.' If using the Birthplace Pass, which allows you entry to this house, Shakespeare's Birthplace, Harvard House and Shakespeare's grave. The cost for an adult ticket is £15.90 for an adult, £9.50 for a child, £14.90 for concessions and £41.50 for families. Tickets allow entry for 12 months.

Opening Times: 16th March until 1st November, 10am until 5pm. 2nd November until 13th March, 11am until 4pm.

Harvard House

This is currently being included in the passes as a place to visit whilst New Place and Nash House are closed for conservation work (reopening in 2016.) Harvard House is a unique Elizabethan town house set over 3 floors.

The house dates back to 1596. It was built by the grandfather of John Harvard, the founder of Harvard University. It is an attractive house with costumes for the children to dress up in.
Harvard House does not have a direct connection with Shakespeare, other than it is of course close to where Shakespeare once lived. It is however an interesting house with friendly and helpful staff. If you have the Birthplace or Five House Pass, it is worth a visit if you have the time.

Getting There: Harvard House is located at 26 The High Street and only a short walk from Shakespeare's Birthplace.

Entry: Harvard House is part of both the 'Five House Pass' and the 'Birthplace Pass.' If using the Birthplace Pass, which allows you entry to this house, Shakespeare's Birthplace, Hall's Croft and Shakespeare's grave. The cost for an adult ticket is £15.90 for an adult, £9.50 for a child, £14.90 for concessions and £41.50 for families. Tickets allow entry for 12 months.

Five Houses Pass
Entry to the properties can be done individually depending on whether you want to see them all or not. If you would like to see all 5 places then there is one ticket that covers them all. The cost is £23.90 for an adult, £14 for a child, £21.90 for concessions and a family ticket is £61.90. There is a 10% discount available when you book online.

Shakespeare Houses and Gardens Pass
Visit any 3 houses from the above 5 for £13.20 (adults), £8.40 (children), £12.40 concessions and £34.80 families. The pass is valid for 1 year. **www.visitbritainshop.com**

FREE APP
Download the free Eye Shakespeare App – **www.itunes.apple.com**

Other Shakespeare Attractions

Shakespeare's Grave

VisitEngland/jameskerr.co.uk

If you've seen Shakespeare's birthplace, you may as well see where he was laid to rest. William Shakespeare died in 1616 and was buried at Holy Trinity Church. The church is worth a visit in its own right, with an elegant spire, located alongside the River Avon.

Shakespeare's final resting place is said to be by the altar, with an inscription, said to be written by Shakespeare himself;

"Good friend for Jesus sake forbeare, to digg the dust encloased heare. blese be the man that spares thes stones, and curst be he that moves my bones."

In other words, don't dig up his bones, or you will be cursed.

Getting There: Holy Trinity Church is located on the River Avon on Old Town, about a 10-15 minute walk from Shakespeare's birth place.

Entry: Admission to Holy Trinity is free. However, if you want to visit Shakespeare's grave you will need to pay £2 (£1 concessions and 50p for students.) If you have either of the passes mentioned above then it is included in your ticket price.

Opening Times: March and October Monday to Saturday 9am – 5pm, Sunday 12.30 – 5pm. April until September Monday to Saturday 8.30am until 6pm, Sunday 12.30 until 5pm. November until February, Monday to Saturday 9am – 4pm, Sunday 12.30 -5pm. Last admission is 20 minutes before closing. The church is closed to visitors on Good Friday, Christmas Day, Boxing Day and New Year's Day.

Royal Shakespeare Company

Photo Credit – VisitEngland/RSC

The internationally acclaimed Royal Shakespeare Company performs the works of Shakespeare throughout the year in Stratford-upon-Avon. The Grade II listed theatre is located on the waterside of the River Avon.

Whether you are a fan of theatre or not, you really should try and visit the RSC here. There are two theatres, the Royal Shakespeare Theatre seating 1,040 people and the Swan Theatre, seating 450 people.

To see a performance take a look at the website to see what is on **www.rsc.org.uk**

Even if you don't have the time to experience a performance, you should still visit. You can go on a Theatre Tour and learn all about the theatre, from the past up until the present day. There is a choice of Front of House, Behind the Scenes, Family Tours, Open Air Tours, After Dark Tours. Tours last about 1 hour (they can be booked in advance online or over the phone **www.rsc.org.uk**)

Take a Tower Tour and enjoy the incredible views across Stratford-upon-Avon. A lift takes you up to the viewing platform and stairs bring you back down again. As you come down, there is an exhibition on the walls. The Tower Tour costs £2.50 per person and £1.25 for under 18s. Advanced booking is recommended here **www.rsc.org.uk**

If you feel like a treat, head on up to the Rooftop Restaurant for afternoon tea (or lunch/dinner) and enjoy the panoramic views. Book a table online here **www.rsc-rooftop-restaurant.co.uk**

For details on the various opening times please see their website: **www.rsc.org.uk**

Other (non Shakespeare) attractions in Stratford Upon Avon

Of course Stratford-upon-Avon is synonymous with the great playwright, but the town is unique and intriguing in its own right too.

The River Avon

VisitEngland/Stratford-upon-Avon

You can take the River Avon Trail, a pleasant walk alongside the canal. Alternatively, you can hop on a canal boat and sit back and enjoy the scenery going by as you listen to the history of the area by an audio tour. Canal & River Tours run regular tours lasting about 45 minutes. The first tour leaves at 11am and the last 4pm. Tours start at Stratford Canal Basin and take you down on to the River Avon.

You can book your boat tour online **www.canalandrivertours.com**

Tickets cost £6 for adults, £4 for children, £5 for concessions and £17.50 for a family.

Shopping

Stratford-upon-Avon is a pleasant town to shop in, with weekly farmers markets and a variety of independent shops alongside high street names.

The MAD Museum

The MAD Museum is a truly fun and unique place to visit, for both adults and children. The museum is a fascinating place to see some impressive mechanical exhibitions, including interactive displays where visitors get to turn handles, press buttons and watch in delight as displays move, make funny noises and light up.

The museum is refreshing in its uniqueness, with over 60 pieces of kinetic art and automata. There are plenty of contraptions and inventions to keep everyone entertained, robots, marble runs. Allow between 1 and 2 hours for visiting the museum.

Opening Times: The museum is open 7 days a week. During the summer (April-September) the museum is open from 10am until 5pm on weekdays and 10am until 5.30pm on weekends and holidays. During the winter months (October-March), the opening hours are 10.30-4.30 weekdays and 10am-5.30pm on weekends and holidays. The museum is closed on Christmas Eve, Christmas Day and Boxing Day with an earlier closing time of 4pm on New Year's Eve and New Year's Day.

Entry: Adult tickets cost £6.80, Child (6-12) £4.50, Concessions £5.50 and family tickets are £19 (2 adults and 2 children.)

Getting There: The MAD Museum is located close to Shakespeare's Birth Place at 4-5 Henley Street, above Lakeland. **www.themadmuseum.co.uk**

Tours

The **City Sightseeing** Hop on Hop Off tour operates in Stratford-upon-Avon and is a great way of getting around the area, allowing you to get on and off at whichever attraction suits you. The tour loop lasts for 60 minutes with departures every 20 minutes in the summer, every 30-60 minutes in the winter. Adult tickets cost £13.50, Child £7, Concessions £11.50, Family £30 (2 adults, 3 children.)
Tickets can be booked online in advance **www.city-sightseeing.com**

Stratford Town Walk

Representing excellent value for money are the popular Stratford Town Walks that run daily from Bancroft Gardens at 11am (Monday to Friday) and 11am and 2pm (Saturday & Sunday.) A guided town walk takes places 365 days a year. Christmas Day tours start at 10.30am. The tours last around 2 hours. Advanced booking is not required.

Adult tickets cost £6, Concessions £5, Children (under 16) £3, under 8 years are free.

The guide will take you through Stratford, passing the houses linked to William Shakespeare. It is worth knowing that with your tour ticket you will receive 2 for 1 entry for the houses – a saving worth making! Other places you will be shown include the Royal Shakespeare Theatres, 15th century timber-framed buildings, the River Avon, the Guild Chapel, Shakespeare's grammar school and a visit to Holy Trinity Church, where William Shakespeare was buried. The tour is an interesting and entertaining one and comes highly recommended.

They also offer a variety of ghost tours, are you brave enough?

Check out their website for details **www.stratfordtownwalk.co.uk**

Eating & Drinking

Old Thatch Tavern – 13th Century classic pub serving traditional food and good ales. Located in the heart of Stratford-Upon-Avon, 300 yards from Shakespeare's birthplace.
www.oldthatchtavernstratford.co.uk – Greenhill Street, Stratford-Upon-Avon – 01789 295216

Hathaway Tearooms – Traditional tea rooms on the High Street in a Grade II listed building.
www.hathawaytearooms.com – 19 High Street, Stratford-Upon-Avon – 01789 264022

In the Area

Warwick Castle – Just 9 miles away from Stratford-upon-Avon. Please see the chapter for **Warwick Castle** for full details.

Getting there from London

Train – Direct trains leave from London Marylebone and take just over 2 hours to reach Stratford-upon-Avon.

Car – From central London the distance is around 100 miles with a journey time of approximately 2 hours. There are some car parks in the town with spaces usually available in the recreation ground. Alternatively there are some park and ride schemes operating. Take a look at this link for car parks and prices **www.visitstratforduponavon.co.uk**

Tour – Golden Tours offer a variety of day trips which include Stratford-upon-Avon. Most of them include many places (for example Stratford, Oxford and The Cotswolds in one day.) They do however offer a Stratford only day trip which is unguided and costs £40 for an adult. This includes return train fares and the City Sightseeing hop on hop off tour. Evan Evans Tours and Premium Tours also offer similar tours.

TWICKENHAM

Photo Credit – VisitEngland/Diana Jarvis

The world's largest stadium dedicated to rugby union can be found in the town of Twickenham, about 10 miles southwest of London on the River Thames.

The stadium now seats 82,000 spectators. The first game was played in 1909 between local sides Richmond and Harlequins. This year, 2015, will see England host the 8th Rugby World Cup, with the final taking place here at Twickenham Rugby Stadium.

Experiencing Twickenham Rugby Stadium
If you are not able to attend a match day (please see here for details on how to get tickets **www.englandrugby.com** then there are plenty of other options to experience the excitement of Twickenham Rugby Stadium.

A Stadium Tour will provide you with a behind the scenes tour of Twickenham, showing you select places around the Stadium. See the royal box, players' tunnel, England dressing room, pitch side walk, hospitality suites, medical room and a fantastic view from the top of the stand. Tour Guides will tell you all about the daily routines of international rugby players.

The cost of the tour is £20 for adults, £15 concessions, £12 children (under 16) and family tickets (2 adults and 3 children) £50. Entry to the World Rugby Museum is included in your tour price. Tours book up quickly so make sure you book in advance. Tours run Tuesday to Sunday. Please check the website for exact times and closures (on match days.)

The World Rugby Museum is perfect for rugby fans. There are permanent galleries with over 25,000 objects on display. Items include match programs, tickets and minute books. There are interactive games for adults and children allowing you to run, scrum, kick and jump. Allow about an hour for the museum.

Entry to the museum only costs £8 for adults, £7 concessions, £6 children under 16 and family tickets £25 (2 adults and 3 children.) The museum is open Tuesday to Saturday from 10am until 5pm and Sundays 11am until 5pm. Please double check the website for closures.

Things to do in the area

Strawberry Hill House – Strawberry Hill was built by Horace Walpole, the son of Britain's first Prime Minister, Sir Robert Walpole. Strawberry is known around the world as a fine example of Georgian Gothic revival architecture. Visit the magical fairytale like house and explore the spectacular rooms. It really is an enchanting experience, and the perfect way to spend an afternoon. Prices start at £10.80 for adults (children go free.) There are a variety of discounts, please see the website for full details. **www.strawberryhillhouse.org.uk**

Getting There From Central London

Train – Trains leave from London Waterloo Station and travel direct to Twickenham Station. The journey takes about 30 minutes. It is a 10 minute walk from the station to the stadium.

Address – Twickenham Stadium, Whitton Road, Twickenham, TW2 7BA.

WARWICK CASTLE

Photo Credit – VisitEngland/jameskerr.co.uk

An incredible medieval castle located in Warwick in the county of Warwickshire, on the bend of the River Avon. The castle was rebuilt in the 12th century, based on the original wooden castle that was built by William the Conqueror in 1068.

Warwick Castle is a beautiful building set within an amazing 64 acres. There is a lot of history to take in at Warwick Castle, dating back to the Saxon times. A day at Warwick Castle really does bring the past to life. It does so in a way that makes it interesting for the children too, meaning everyone has a good day!

Exploring Warwick Castle
Daily shows are put on, including a fantastic birds of prey show, where eagles and vultures will fly from the ramparts or maybe a condor just above your head!

Young children will love the Princess Tower where they will be given robes at the start and then asked to help the Princess solve a riddle.

Other shows include the Bowman Show (an archer will show you the techniques and equipment that was used during this popular historic past time.)

The ramparts and towers have incredible views – there are some tight and narrow steps to climb up before you get there (be aware if you are claustrophobic), and there are hundreds of them, but you are rewarded at the top.

Inside the castle, the main hall and rooms opposite are stunning. The interior is grand and rich in history. A tour of the castle is included in your ticket price, check at the entrance for the tour times of that day. The Dungeon Tour is an optional extra, an interactive experience with actors reenacting the gory days of the past. This tour really isn't for those with a nervous disposition – it is scary, and not suitable for young children.

Don't miss the island across the River Avon. You will see the brave knights face each other during the seasonal jousting tournaments. This is also where the firing of the trebuchet takes place.

Peacock Garden and the Grounds
Peacocks are always a beautiful sight, and they seem to fit right in at Warwick Castle. The stunning peacocks roams around in their garden, amongst the perfectly manicured hedges and pretty pond and fountain.

Spare some time for the stunning Rose Garden, first laid down in 1868. If you are there in late June to late July you should see the roses in full bloom.

If you have kids with you then make sure you head for the Pageant Playground, if they've any energy left, here is the place to use it up!

There are plenty of places to picnic within the grounds, or there are a selection of places to eat and drink within Warwick Castle. Take a look at the website to see any special discounts that might be running. **www.warwick-castle.com**

Admission –The Castle Ticket (Castle Entry, Attractions, Grounds and Shows)
Adult (12+) £24.60 on the day, £18.45 online (with Dungeon Tour £29.40 on day, £22.05 online)
Child (4-11) £21.60 on the day, £16.30 online (£24.60 on day, £18.45 online)
Senior (60+) £17.40 on the day, £13.05 online (£21.60 on day, £16.20 online)
Family Tickets are available offering further discounts.

Money Saver Tip – If you travel by train you can get a 2 for 1 entry. Just show your ticket at the gates and printed out voucher from **www.daysoutguide.co.uk**

Open – The castle is open all year round except Christmas Day. From April to September the opening hours are 10am until 6pm, and October to March they are 10am to 5pm.

Recommended Time
At least 4 to 5 hours but to fully appreciate the castle, grounds and shows, at least 1 day. If you want to do everything, then allow even longer.

Eat & Drink

Thomas Oken Tea Rooms – Built 500 years ago by Thomas Oken, the Mayor of the town at the time. Today, the beautiful house is home to tea rooms offering over thirty different teas. The tea rooms also serve delicious cakes and savoury snacks and meals. The tea rooms are licensed and serve local ciders, ales and wines. With outdoor seating available, and located just outside Warwick Castle walls, it is an ideal stop for a refuel.
www.thomasokentearooms.co.uk

Getting There From London

Car – 95 miles from central London, taking about 1 hour and 45 minutes via the M40. Car parking is available at a charge according to which one you use. If you get there later on in the morning be prepared to walk a bit further from the car park to the castle. Please see their page here for different locations and costs **www.warwick-castle.com**

Train – Direct trains go from London Marylebone to Warwick Train Station and takes about 1 hour and 20 minutes. The castle is a 1 mile sign posted walked away.

Tour Company – Evan Evans Tours offer a Warwick Castle, Scenic Cotswolds Drive, Stratford Upon Avon (Shakespeare) and a walking tour of Oxford for £84 (adults) £74 (children) and £79 (concessions.) Premier Tours & Golden Tours all run similar day trips including the same experiences.

WEMBLEY

VisitEngland/Diana Jarvis

A visit to the world famous home of English football is an absolute must for any fan. Experience the excitement of being within the stadium where so many unforgettable sporting moments have taken place.

Immerse yourself in the history of Wembley Stadium, see the 1966 World Cup crossbar, visit the England Changing Rooms (minus the players!), the Press Conference Room or pretend to be a world class footballer as you walk through the Players Tunnel (to the sound of the FIFA music!) and climb the 107 steps to the Royal Box and have your photo taken with a replica FA Cup Trophy.

There are plenty of opportunities to take some fantastic photos whilst learning all you can about the history of the stadium, led by a knowledgeable tour guide for approximately 75 minutes.

Even if you are not a passionate football fan, I think you will still love the experience and feel the sense of excitement of being in a place that has been witness to so many historical events over the years.

If you want to experience a bit more from your tour you can choose the VIP Access All Areas Tour. You will have your own private tour guide who will take you to places not accessible on the normal stadium tour. You will be given complimentary soft drinks when you arrive, a Wembley Tour Guidebook and a gift.

Recommended Time
The normal tour lasts around 75 minutes, but can often go over, so allow a bit of extra time. The VIP Tour is for 2 hours. There is also a Stadium Store that you might want to visit, and allow some time to see the

1948 Olympic Tablets that are located outside the Stadium Store. These historical items have been kept from the Empire Stadium. See all the gold medal winners names engraved on the tablets.

Tickets

Standard Tour tickets cost £19 for an adult, £11 for a child (under 16), £11 for seniors (over 60), £45 for a family ticket and under 5's are free.

The VIP Tour tickets cost £55 each.

You are able to buy your tickets on the day, but it is strongly recommended that you book in advance here **www.wembleystadium.com** or call the booking line on 0844 800 2755.

Money Saving Tip – If travelling by train you can make use of the 2 for 1 entry. Download your voucher here **www.daysoutguide.co.uk/wembley-stadium-tour**

In the Area

If shopping is your thing, then make sure you visit the nearby **London Designer Outlet**, with discounts of up to 70% off the recommended retail price. There are 50 outlets from the high street alongside restaurants, a play park and a 9 screen cinema complex. **www.londondesigneroutlet.com**

Getting There From London

The easiest way to get to Wembley Stadium is using public transport.

Train – Catch a train from London Marylebone to Wembley Stadium. The journey time is just 9 minutes.
Tube – Wembley Park is on both the Jubilee and Metropolitan underground.

Further Information
www.wembleystadium.com Wembley Stadium, Wembley, London HA9 0WS – Tel 0844 800 2755

WHITSTABLE

VisitEngland/Diana Jarvis

Whitstable is a popular seaside town about 5 miles north of Canterbury, on the north coast of Kent. The town dates back to before the writing of the Domesday Book and has a rich maritime history. Whitstable is famous for its oysters which have been collected in the area since the Roman times. There is an Oyster Festival each year in July.

Whitstable is well known for its wonderful fish restaurants and pubs. There are a wide range of independent craft and gift shops as well as galleries and other foods shops.

Things to do in Whitstable

Whitstable Harbour
The harbour is not far from the train station. It was opened in 1831 when there was once a railway service operating from London all the way to the harbour.

Whitstable Harbour is an interesting place to explore with an inviting buzz as you wander past the varied market stalls and wooden huts selling crafts and fresh sea food.

Located on the South Quay and close to the fishing boats is the Whitstable Harbour Village. Open every weekend and bank holiday from 10am to 5pm and on week days during high season. The village is home to local producers and independent local suppliers.

If you are there between 23rd July and 3rd August in 2015, don't miss the Whitstable Oyster Festival, now in its 31st year. Many events are put on to celebrate the town's famous oysters, and of course, many oysters are sold and consumed!
www.whitstableoysterfestival.co.uk

Whitstable Town Centre
Whitstable is a fantastic little town to walk through for its quirky and independent little shops. Full of character and charm, there are gift shops, antique shops, clothing boutiques and if you have a sweet tooth, see if you can sniff out The Sugar Boy on Harbour Street for some old fashioned sweets.

One main street makes up Whitstable, if you arrive by train start at the beginning of Oxford Street and follow the road down into the High Street and then Harbour Street where the majority of the art galleries and boutique shops can be found.

Tankerton Beach & Tankerton Slopes
A lovely clean pebble beach with clear water (should you wish to take a dip), about a 1 mile walk along the sea wall from Whitstable. With pretty multi coloured beach huts, Tankerton beach is a nice spacious spot to appreciate the sea views and Kent coastline.

When it is low tide you can walk out to sea along 'the street' and explore the rock pools – just make sure you keep an eye on when the tide is coming back in, or you may find yourself suddenly surrounded by lots of water!

Tankerton Slopes is a popular green area where the slopes lead down to Tankerton beach below. The slopes are popular year round with families, dog walkers, cyclists and people having picnics. In the summer the slopes are used for the regatta's fireworks display along with the community fun day.

When walking between Tankerton Slopes and Whitstable you can make a stop off at Whitstable Castle and enjoy the beautiful gardens.

Where to Eat & Drink in Whitstable
Whitstable has an incredible range of quality places to eat and drink it doesn't seem fair to only name a few, but, in the interest of space, I have had to narrow it down to the following;

Tankerton Arms – A well run and friendly pub in Tankerton serving a good range of local beers from local microbreweries and local ciders and wine. The Tankerton Arms is a real gem and definitely worth a visit if you enjoy quality beer in a great atmosphere. Please check the website for varied opening hours (it is closed on Mondays.)

139B Tankerton Road, (B2205), Tankerton, Whitstable, Kent CT5 2AW – **www.thetankertonarms.co.uk** – 07532 025626

Wheelers Oyster Bar – The oldest restaurant in town, Wheelers Oyster Bar comes highly recommended. They have an a la carte menu, changing seasonally and a browsing menu where you can pick from a selection of seafood dishes. There are 4 sittings a day starting at 1pm, 3pm, 5pm and last orders at 7.30pm, except on a Sunday when the last order is at 7pm. Wheelers is a bring your own bottle restaurant with an off license opposite selling both local and international wines. Booking in advance is recommended.

8 High Street, Whitstable CT5 1BQ – **www.wheelersoysterbar.com** – tel: 01227 273311

Samphire – A great little bistro, perfect for a spot of brunch. All dishes are locally sourced. They are open 7 days a week, serving brunch, lunch and supper. Phone ahead on 01227 770075 for reservations.

4 High Street, Whitstable – **www.letseat.at/SamphireWhitstable**

Sundae Sundae – Not far from the harbour is the delicious Sundae Sundae ice cream bar, serving a tempting range of traditional English ice creams and lollies alongside some sweet treats in the ice cream delicatessen.

62 Harbour Street, Whitstable, Kent, CT5 1AG – **www.sundaesundae.co.uk**

Getting to Whitstable from London

Train – Southeastern run direct trains from London St Pancras (1hr13) and London Victoria (1hr25) to Whitstable.

Car – Whitstable is about 60 miles from central London. The journey should take about 1 hour and 20 minutes, depending on traffic, via the M2 and A2. There are a number of pay and display car parks and parking bays in Whitstable. If you want a full list please see the map here **www.canterbury.gov.uk**

WIMBLEDON

For two weeks every June, Wimbledon wins the hearts of tennis lovers across the world. Even those who don't normally follow tennis get swept up in the excitement of the tournament, even if just an excuse to eat more strawberries and cream (the traditional food of the Wimbledon Championships!)

The Wimbledon Championships is one of the most famous tennis tournaments in the world. It is the oldest, having been held at the All England Club in Wimbledon since 1877.

Wimbledon is the only Grand Slam still played on grass, hence its original name, lawn tennis.

The Wimbledon Tennis Museum and Tour is a must do if you have any interest in tennis.

The 90 minute Wimbledon Experience is led by an informative tour guide, taking you close to where all the action is, to all the well-known places within the Wimbledon enclosure. Visit the famous centre court, the media centre, players' area, Henman Hill and the locker rooms. Walk in the footsteps of famous tennis players from the past up to the present day.

The museum itself has lots of memorabilia from the history of tennis dating back to 1555, all the way up to today's championship trophy.

See the evolution of the tennis racket, from the original wooden ones up to the more modernly designed rackets used by the tennis champions today.

On display are the outfits worn by some of the tennis greats, including Pete Sampras, Martina Navratilova, Roger Federa and Andy Murray.

The 'ghost' of John McEnroe (he is a holographic) takes you on a journey of tennis in the same changing room he used!

There is a 3D cinema showing the science of tennis and an interactive area including touch screen consoles.

There is an audio guide included in the ticket price (in 10 languages) to help add to the experience whilst you walk around the museum.

Recommended Time
If doing both the tour and the museum, allow around 2 and a half hours. Use the rest of the day to enjoy the pretty village of Wimbledon.

Tickets

Museum Only – Adults £13, Concessions £11, Children (5-16) £8

Museum & Tour – Adults £24, Concessions £21, Children £15

The tour is a very popular event so it is recommended that you book in advance. You can do so via their **online booking** or by calling them on 020 8946 6131.

The museum is open from 10am until 1730 daily. Please see the above online booking facility for available tour times.

The tour and museum is closed on 24th/25th December, 1st January and during the Wimbledon Tournament. Please check on their website.

Money Saving Tip 1 – If you have a London Pass, entry to both the museum and the tour is included. Please see the **Passes and Discounts** chapter for details.

Money Saving Tip 2 – If you travel by train you can use the 2 for 1 entry voucher, download it here **www.daysoutguide.co.uk/wimbledon-lawn-tennis-museum**

In the Area
Although Wimbledon is mostly known for the tennis championships, there is much more to the town (or village as it is called.) It is well worth combining your visit to the museum with an explore around the area.

If the weather is treating you well, pack a picnic and head to Wimbledon Common, you might even spot a Womble! **Wimbledon Common** is a wonderful open space with lots of woodland, nature trails, and a pond.

Visit the **Wimbledon Windmill Museum** where children can mill some of their own flour. The windmill dates back to 1817 and is a distinctive landmark in the area, now providing an interesting insight to windmills, milling and local history. Please note the museum is only open at weekends and on bank holidays from April to October. Admission to the museum is £2 per adult, £1 per child and concessions. **www.wimbledonwindmill.org.uk**

The first Buddhist Temple in the UK is in Wimbledon. Visit the **Buddhapadipa Temple** and grounds which covers 4 acres, including an ornamental lake, a flower garden and orchard. Entry is free. The temple grounds are open to the public every day from 9am until 6pm, but the main temple is only open to the public on weekends. **www.buddhapadipa.org**

The village of Wimbledon itself is a pretty leafy suburb of London. With independent shops and fine dining, pubs and cafes, it is worth a stroll down the high street before you return back to central London.

Getting There From London
The easiest way to get to Wimbledon from central London is using public transport.

Train – Regular trains run from London Waterloo to Wimbledon Station. It is a 15 minute walk from the station.

Tube – Take the District Line (westbound) to either Southfields (a 15 minute walk from the grounds) or Wimbledon (a 20 minute walk from the grounds.) If you would rather not walk you can either take a taxi or the General London Shuttle bus from Wimbledon station.

Further   Information
www.wimbledon.com The All England Lawn Tennis Club, Church Road, Wimbledon, London SW19 5AE - Telephone: 020 8946 6131

WINCHESTER

Winchester, England's ancient capital, is bursting with a rich and varied history. Once the seat of King Alfred the Great, whose statue you can see in the centre of the town. The River Itchen flows through the town, with a wide selection of independent shops, restaurants, cafes and bars.

The city of Winchester is located on the edge of the South Downs National Park, combining a perfect mix of rural beauty with a vibrant city. It is a compact town, meaning getting about on foot is relatively easy.

Winchester Cathedral

Top of most visitor's list is the magnificent and world famous Winchester Cathedral. The Cathedral is Europe's longest medieval Cathedral, with over 1,000 years of history. Aside from the stunning architecture, there is plenty to see, including the famed 12th century Winchester Bible.

For literary fans, Winchester Cathedral is the resting place of Jane Austen, who lived in the nearby village of Chawton (see further on for details on visiting Jane Austen's house.) Originally there was no mention of Austen's literary achievements on the memorial tomb, this was later rectified in 1872 when a brass plaque was added and later in 1900, a stained glass window, in acknowledgement of her literacy fame.

A modern memorial marks the spot where the tomb of St Swithun once was. St Swithun was an Anglo-Saxon Bishop, a century after his death he was chosen as the patron saint of Cathedral's Benedictine Monastery. Sadly, his tomb was destroyed during Henry VIII's reign. Learn all about the fascinating history and legend of St Swithun at the Cathedral.

If you can, it is well worth taking one of the Cathedral tours, included in your admission price. A trained Cathedral guide can explain the incredible history and facts of the Cathedral. The tours last between 1 hour – 1.5 hours and run Monday to Saturday on the hours from 10am until 3pm.

One of the oldest parts of the Cathedral is the Crypt. A 20 minute tour of the Crypt is also included in your admission price and they run at 10.30, 12.30 and 2.30pm.

The Tower Tour is an additional cost should you wish to climb the 213 steps to the top. You will be greeted with amazing views of Winchester and the surrounding countryside. The tour prices is £6 and lasts around 1.5 hours. Tower Tours are not suitable for those under the age of 12 or those afraid of heights and small spaces. To find out the tour times and to book please call 01962 857 275.

If you wish to go on a self-guided audio tour, they are available at a cost of £3 (45 minutes – 1.5 hours) and are available at the Entrance Desk.

There are many events and activities held during the year, including exhibitions, classical concerts, and at Christmas time a large market and ice rink.

There is a cafe at the Cathedral with an open-air terrace and garden where you can recharge with a delicious pastry, lunch or Hampshire cream tea.

There is a shop selling souvenirs, including CDs of the Cathedral Choir.

Admission – The Cathedral, crypt and treasury are open Monday to Saturday from 9.30am to 5pm. Sundays, 12.30 to 3pm. Please check on the website before you visit for any temporary closures.

The cost of entry is £7.50 for adults, £5 concessions and £4 students. Children (with family) are free. Your ticket allows you to visit as many times as you wish within a 12 month period. A children's trail is included in the admission price, providing families a fun way to learn about the Cathedral's history.

Tours of the Cathedral are included in your entry price and are every hour from 10am until 3pm. Tours of the crypt are at 10.30am, 12.30pm and 2.30pm, Monday to Saturday.

A Tower Tour is an additional £6 and an Audio Tour is £3.

Evensong takes place Monday to Saturday at 5.30pm and on a Sunday at 3.30pm.

Further Information – www.winchester-cathedral.org.uk – 9 The Close, Hampshire, SO23 9LS

King Arthur's Round Table in the Great Hall
The legendary Arthurian Round Table is an incredible sight, found in the Great Hall, at the top of Winchester High Street.

This is, apparently, where King Arthur and his Knights of the Round Table met. Learn all about the fascinating history of the Round Table

The Great Hall, originally built for William the Conqueror in 1067, is all that remains of Winchester Castle.

The Great Hall is open daily from 10am until 5pm but does occasionally close to the public so please check the website before you visit. The cost to enter is a suggested donation of £3 per person.

Further Information – www3.hants.gov.uk – Castle Avenue, Winchester, Hampshire, SO23 8PJ

Westgate Museum
The fortified gateway once served as a debtor's prison (you can see graffiti from the prisoners on the walls) and is the last of the main medieval gates into the city. A visit to the listed monument will showcase Winchester's Tudor and Stuart period, with a great collection of weights and measures.

Children can try on a suit of armour or make an authentic brass rubbing (for a small fee.)

Entry to Westgate Museum is free with varying opening times. Please see the website for full details.
www.winchester.gov.uk

Westgate Museum, High Street, Winchester, So23 9AP

St Giles' Hill

For some fantastic panoramic views of the city's landscape and landmarks, a short climb up St Giles' Hill is well worth it. You can even spy the statue of King Alfred the Great when you are up there. A great spot for a picnic.

Statue of King Alfred the Great

King Alfred the Great was a significant and fascinating King. He ruled Wessex from 871 until his death in 899. King Alfred was a soldier, scholar and statesman, achieving many remarkable acts during his life, earning him the title of 'The Great One.' You can go on a self-guided tour of King Alfred's Winchester, starting at Winchester Tourist Information.

Details can be downloaded here **www.visitwinchester.co.uk** The Broadway, Winchester, SO23 9GH

Winchester City Museum

Located adjacent to the Cathedral, the museum is home to three galleries, each telling the unique and fascinating story of Winchester. The museum is brilliant for families with lots of interactive activities for the children to enjoy.

An audio guide is available in English, Spanish and French.

Entry to the museum is free and is open daily. Opening hours vary, please visit the website for exact times. **www.winchester.gov.uk**

Winchester City Museum, The Square, Winchester, Hampshire SO23 9ES

Winchester College

Winchester College is thought to be the oldest continuously running school in England. It was founded in 1382 by the Bishop of Winchester at that time (William Wykeham.)

Around 700 boys between the ages of 13 to 18 are taught at the college today.

You are only able to access the college on a guided tour. The tours take you to the medieval parts of the college. The tours cost £7 for adults and £6 for concessions. As it is a working college, please check on the website for tour dates and time.

www.winchestercollege.org Winchester College, College Street, Winchester SO23 9NA

Winchester City Mill

Winchester City Mill is a National Trust owned property, a unique and rare example of an urban working corn mill. It is powered by the River Itchen which passes under the mill. Visitors can enjoy hands-on activities learn about the history of the working watermill.

Adult entry is £4, Child £2 and Family £10. Opening times vary, please visit the website for details. **www.nationaltrust.org.uk** Winchester City Mill, Bridge St, Winchester, Hampshire SO23 0EJ

Military Museums

Opposite The Great Hall are a group of 5 military museums including The Gurkha Museum, The Royal Green Jackets (Rifles) Museum, The Royal Hampshire Regiment Museum, The Guardroom Museum and Horsepower. Each museum is independently run with entry to The Gurkha Museum costing from £3 and The Royal Greens from £3.75. The other three museums are free to enter. Opening hours vary for each museum, further information can be found here **www.winchestermilitarymuseums.co.uk**

Hospital of St Cross

A 20 minute walk from the Winchester City centre, set in the water meadows by the River Itchen, is the ancient Grade I listed buildings of The Hospital of St Cross. They date back to 1132 and showcase admirable medieval architecture.

The Hospital of St Cross is a private foundation and retreat which has provided food and shelter for hundreds of years. To this day, they still provide individual apartments for a community of around 25 elderly men, known as 'Brothers.' However, they welcome visitors to experience the unique medieval buildings, the Victorian Old Kitchen, meat room, cellar and extensive gardens.

Unique to the Hospital of St Cross is the ancient tradition of providing the Wayfarer's Dole – you may request this at the Porter's Lodge as you leave!

There is a gift shop at the Porter's Lodge and a Tea Room in the Hundred Men's Hall.

Admission costs £4 for adults, £3.50 for concessions and £2 for children under the age of 13. For opening times please see the website **www.hospitalofstcross.co.uk**

Hospital of St Cross, Saint Cross Back Street, Winchester, Hampshire SO23 9SD

Wolvesey Castle

Visit the ruins of Wolvesey Castle, located next to Winchester Cathedral. An importance residence of the wealthy and powerful Bishops of Winchester since Anglo-Saxon times.

Admission to Wolvesey Castle is free. A free audio guide is available for download on the website. **www.english-heritage.org.uk**

Wolvesey Castle is open from April until November daily from 10am until 5pm. Please see the website to check. **www.english-heritage.org.uk** Wolvesey Castle, Winchester, Hampshire SO23 9ND

The English Romantic Poet, John Keats

The world famous English poet, John Keats wrote his famous 'Ode To Autumn' whilst staying in Winchester. Download the self-guided route that Keats took each day and inspired him to pen the above poem.

The walk is roughly 2 miles in length.

The round trip is approximately two miles. Pavements, paths and grass lie underfoot and stout shoes are advisable after wet weather.

Download the trip route from **www.visitwinchester.co.uk/keats-walk**

Tours of Winchester

A great way to get to know the best bits of Winchester is to take one of the tours.

Self-Guided Walks – Visit Winchester provide a selection of free to download walks including a City Walk, Sunset Walk, Keats Walk, among others. **www.visitwinchester.co.uk**

Official Tour – There are a wide choice of special interest tours alongside regular tours of the city, run by Winchester's enthusiastic and qualified tourist guides.

Regular tours leave from the tourist information centre and last about 90 minutes. Adult tickets cost £5 and accompanying children are free.

The Tourist Information Centre recommend advanced booking of tours on 01962 840 500 or **tourism@winchester.gov.uk**

In the Area

Chawton

For fans of Jane Austen, a visit to the Jane Austen Museum in Chawton, 17 miles away, is recommended. Austen lived there from 1809 until 1817 and wrote several of her novels there, including Emma and Sense and Sensibility. The museum showcases some of Jane's personal belongings alongside original manuscripts and a bookcase with Austen's first editions. You can explore the house where she lived with her mother and sister, for the last 8 years of her life, before she passed away in Winchester.

Entry is £8 for adults, £6.50 for concessions, and £3 for children (6 to 16.) Please check the website for opening times.

Further information – **www.jane-austens-house-museum.org.uk**

Stonehenge

A further 40 minute drive along the A303 will bring you to the world famous site of Stonehenge. Of course, Stonehenge can also be combined with a visit to Bath or Salisbury, so you might want to save it for that. Please see the **chapter on Stonehenge** for more information.

Getting to Winchester from London

Train – There are direct trains from London Waterloo to Winchester, the fastest journey time taking just under an hour. A walk from the station to the cathedral takes no longer than 10 minutes.

Car – Winchester is just under 70 miles from central London, and on a clear run, you can drive it in 1 hour and 35 minutes via the M3. If you want to make a divert to Chawton then you can take the A3 out of London and reach Chawton in around 1 hour and 20 minutes. The onward drive to Winchester is a further 16 miles on the A31 (approx. 25 minutes.) There are numerous pay and display and pay on foot car parks in Winchester, with free parking available on Sundays. There are also 3 park and ride car parks, details of which can be found here. **www.winchester.gov.uk**

WINDSOR & ETON

Credit VisitEngland/Doug Harding

Windsor Castle is probably one of the most well-known castles and Royal residences in England, if not the world. It is certainly the oldest and largest inhabited castle in the world. The original castle was built by William the Conqueror, after the Norman invasion. It has since been occupied by each succeeding monarch.

Windsor Castle

The official residence of Her Majesty The Queen, and previously the family home of British Kings and Queens for almost 1,000 years. Windsor Castle is a great part of British History and one I wouldn't want to miss – just think what those walls have seen and heard over the years!

The Queen spends much of her time at Windsor Castle, with many private weekends and official residences throughout the year. The Castle is frequently used for State and ceremonial occasions, with many State visits hosted here.

What to see

– Start your visit off with a **Precincts Tour,** a free 30 minute tour of the Castle Precincts, led by the Wardens. They leave at regular intervals from the Courtyard.

– **The State Apartments** are a reflection of the various different monarchs that have occupied them over the years. With stunning works of art from the Royal Collection, including paintings by Rembrandt, Ruben and Canaletto. The State Apartments are used today by members of the Royal Family for various different events.

– **Queen Mary's Dolls' House** was built for Queen Mary between 1921 and 1924 and is the largest and most famous dolls' house in the world. The incredibly detailed house is fascinating to see with thousands of items carefully made in intricate detail on a tiny scale of 1:12. Incredibly, the Dolls' House has running hot and cold water, working lifts, flushing lavatories and electricity!

– **The Semi-State Rooms** are used by The Queen for official entertaining. The incredible private apartments are open between September and March.

– **St George's Chapel** holds the tombs of ten previous monarchs, including Henry VIII and his third wife Jane Seymour and Charles I. Visitors are welcome to attend services that take place at least three times a day. It is however closed to visitors on Sundays.

– **Changing the Guard**

Photo Credit – VisitEngland/Doug Harding

Often at the top of many visitors must see events. Changing the Guard takes place inside the Castle Precincts, usually at 11am. From April until the end of July it is daily from Monday to Saturday, and every other day for the rest of the year. The ceremony takes 45 minutes.

Guides

– A free app is available to download via the app store is a 'Capturing Windsor Castle' featuring a collection of watercolour paintings and contemporary pictures showcasing Windsor Castle and the grounds. **www.itunes.apple.com**

– A free multimedia tour is available to pick up in the Courtyard at the start of your tour. The tour guides you through the castle where you will learn about the history of the castle from the days of William the Conqueror through to the present day. The self-guided tour takes about 2 hours. A family multimedia tour is also available, aimed at children between the ages of 7 and 11.

Tours

– A number of tours are available at the castle. To find out more and to book please see them all listed here **www.royalcollection.org.uk**

– Special **'Conquer the Tower Tour'** takes place between Saturday 1st August 2015 and Wednesday 30th September 2015. Visitors can climb the 200 steps to the top of Windsor Castle's iconic Round Tower. Just don't forget your camera for a panoramic picture of those incredible views of the Thames Valley, London skyline and of course Windsor Castle. You will also be able to get up close to the Castle's 15 metre flagpole. If the Royal Standard is flying, The Queen is in residence, if the Union Flag is flying, then The Queen is away from Windsor.

Special combined tickets are available for entry to Windsor Castle and the 'Conquer the Tower Tour.' Adult tickets cost £27.70, Concessions £24.70, under 17/Disabled £16.90, Under 5s free, Family (2 adults, 3 children) £71.30. Allow about 45 minutes for the climb. It is available 10.15am and 4.05pm every day.

Recommended Time

Allow about 3 hours to see all of Windsor Castle.

Admission Adult tickets cost £19.50, Concessions £17.50, under 17/Disabled £11.30, Under 5s are free, and Family Tickets (2 adults and 3 children) cost £49.70. When the state apartments are closed, the entrance fee is reduced. If you buy your ticket directly from Royal Collection Trust (either online or on the day) you can turn your entry ticket into a 1 year pass.

Money Saving Tip – Entry to Windsor Castle is included in your London Pass, including the Fast Track, so no waiting in the queue! (Please see the chapter on **Passes & Discounts**.)

Opening – From March until October, daily openings from 9.45am until 5.15pm (last admission 4pm.) From November to February, daily openings from 9.45am until 4.15pm (last admission 3pm.) Please note the castle is closed on 15th June 2015. The State Apartments are closed on various days, please check the website to confirm. The Semi State Rooms are only open during winter months (September to March.)

Address – Windsor Castle, Windsor, Berkshire SL4 1NJ

Contact – www.royalcollection.org.uk or Ticket Sales & Information on +44 (0)20 7766 7304.

Other Attractions in Royal Windsor

Windsor Castle is a huge draw to the area, and rightly so, but the surrounding area is worth an explore too. With plenty to see, either on an organised tour or by yourself. There are some lovely pubs and independent shops to explore, so make sure you leave some time for them!

Savill Garden

Take an international journey through the world class Savill Garden in Windsor Great Park.

The Savill Garden, is an elegant combination of traditional British horticulture with contemporary garden design where thousands of beautiful plants from all over the world are arranged in exciting and innovative schemes. Set in thirty-five acres in the heart of Windsor Great Park, it is a garden for all seasons where visitors are welcome to explore the meandering paths and interconnecting gardens throughout the year.

The Garden was created by Sir Eric Savill in the 1930's with the support of King George V and Queen Mary. Since then the Garden has continued to develop under royal patronage with HM The Queen opening the Rose Garden in 2010.

Enjoy an international journey with a worldwide selection of plants including the Dry Garden which draws its inspiration from the natural habitats of the Mediterranean basin; the New Zealand Garden which showcases nearly 3,000 New Zealand plants and builds on the gift of a collection of native plants given to Her Majesty The Queen following a state visit in 1986; together with many stunning plants throughout the Garden from Japan and China.

Highlights of the Garden also include the internationally renowned colourful spring displays of azaleas, magnolias and rhododendrons; the award winning summer Rose Garden with 2,500 scented roses planted within a spectacular palette of colours radiating out from an intense centre of deep plum through soft pinks fading to white and subtle apricots to tangerine orange; the autumn colour with Japanese maples forming the backbone of The Savill Garden displays, their leaves varying in colour from butter yellow, to orange and red; and winter with swathes of colourful willows, dogwoods, and the National Collection of Mahonias.

Following a refreshing walk, visit The Savill Garden Restaurant or the Gallery Coffee Shop in The Savill Building, where you can enjoy freshly made coffee and homemade cakes.

Admission – Adults £8.75, Seniors £8.75, Child (6-16) £4.35, Family £26 (2 adults, 2 children) the garden is free to enter during December, January and February.

Opening – Savill Garden is open all year, closing on Christmas Eve and Christmas Day. During the summer season (1st March – 31st October) the opening times are 10am until 6pm daily (last admission 5.30pm) and during the winter months the opening times are 10am until 4.30pm (last admission 4pm.)

Address – The Great Park, Windsor, Berkshire, SL4 2HT

Contact – For more information call 01784 435400 or visit **www.theroyallandscape.co.uk**

Windsor Great Park

Photo Credit – VisitEngland/Doug Harding

Part of the Windsor Estate and managed by the Crown Estate, it is easily accessible from Windsor town Centre by going down the Long Walk. The Long Walk starts at Windsor Castle (Cambridge Gates) and runs for 2.65 miles until you reach the monument of the Copper Horse. If you fancy something a little bit different, you can always travel down the Long Walk in a horse and carriage, see the section further on in this chapter for details.

The ideal place to go for a picnic or a relaxing stroll. Windsor Great Park spans an area of 4,800 acres, with a mix of woodlands, open grasslands, ancient oaks, deer, a lake and some incredible views.

Windsor Great Park incorporates The Savill Gardens (above), The Valley Gardens and Virginia Water Lake.

There really is a huge amount of space to cover so it is worth downloading a map before you go to decide what you want to see; **www.theroyallandscape.co.uk**

Admission – Free to enter (apart from The Savill Gardens)

Opening – All year from 7am until dusk.

Address – Windsor Great Park

Contact – www.theroyallandscape.co.uk

River Thames Boat Trip

If you are able, the 40 minute round boat trip on the River Thames with French Brothers is a fantastic way to get a great view of Windsor Castle and Eton College. Boats depart at regular intervals throughout the day. Longer trips are available, please see their website for details.

Admission – Adult £7 (online £6.20), Child £4.65 (online £4.10), Senior £6.30 (online £5.55), Family (2 adults and 2 children) £18.65 (online £16.40), Family (2 adults and 3 children) £20.90 (online £18.40.)

Money Saving Tip – If you have a London Pass you can get a 20% discount on French Brothers trips

Opening – From February 14th until November 1st the trips run from 10am until 5pm. During other times they run on weekends only.

Address – Windsor Promenade Barry Avenue, Windsor, Berkshire, SL4 1QX

Contact – **www.frenchbrothers.co.uk** or **sales@boat-trips.co.uk** or telephone on 01753 851900

Eton

Eton is a small detour across the Thames River Bridge from Windsor and worthy of an explore. The charming High Street and of course the historical and world famous Eton College. Enjoy a walk around the cobbled streets in the village and peek in the small picturesque shops and pubs. There are book shops, antique shops, flower shops and other delightfully quaint places to discover.

Eton College – At the time of writing this guide, Eton College were not open for public visitors due to building work. The estimated opening time is late 2015/early 2016, so you might want to check on their website. However, depending on when you are visiting, you might well see some students dressed in their suits and tails.

Eton College is about a 15 minute walk from Windsor. Eton College is the oldest boarding school for boys in England and has seen 19 Prime Ministers alongside many Kings and Princes of England graduate over the years. Eton was founded in 1441 by Henry IV.

Eton College Natural History Museum

Housed in a beautiful building at the end of Eton High Street is a small yet very interesting museum, dating back to 1875. The unique Eton College Natural History Museum has some great exhibitions including some on dinosaurs, fossils, birds and all kinds of flora and fauna. Well worth a visit.

Admission – Free

Opening – On Sunday afternoons from 2.30pm until 5pm.

Address – The Curator, Natural History Museum, Eton College, Windsor, SL4 6DW

Contact – **www.etonnhm.com** or 01753 671288 or **etonnhm@etoncollege.org.uk**

Self-Guided Heritage Trail

You can download a free Heritage Trail from the official Windsor Tourism website. The self-guided trail encompasses the historic parts of Windsor, around the walls of Windsor Castle, then down towards and over the River Thames and into Eton. **www.windsor.gov.uk**

Royal Windsor Town Walks

If you are here on a Saturday or Sunday between Easter and the end of September, you can go on a Royal Windsor Town Walk with a professional Blue Badge Guide.

The tour runs on a Saturday at 11.30am and Sunday at 2.30pm. The tours last for just over an hour and meet at Royal Windsor Information Centre.

Horse Drawn Carriage Rides

Introduced by Queen Victoria in 1849, travelling around Windsor in the comfort of a horse-drawn hackney carriage is a longstanding tradition.

You can go on a circular route from outside the castle walls on Castle Hill, opposite the Queen Victoria statue at the top of the High Street.

I mentioned earlier on in the Windsor Great Park section about an alternative to walking The Long Walk. Orchard Poyle offer 'The Long Walk Experience' which is a 30 minute round trip. The only way to go down Long Walk is either on foot or Horse Drawn Hackney Carriages, this has been in place since 1849. The cost for this experience is £40 per carriage and seats either 4 or 6 people, depending on the carriage. There is no need to book. If you call at 9am on the day to check that they are in town. Tours run from midday outside the castle.

Contact – Call on 07803 720084 or visit **www.orchardpoyle.co.uk**

Hop on Hop off City Sightseeing Open Top Bus

A circular route lasting 1 hour, taking in Windsor and Eton. The tour runs from March until October every 30 minutes. Adult tickets cost £12.50, Child £6, Concessions £10.50 and Family £29. **www.city-sightseeing.com**

Windsor Duck Tours

Mix a bit of water with your land adventure – the amphibious buses take you round Windsor before plunging into the River Thames for some alternative views of Windsor Castle and Eton. A real fun and unique way to do it.

There are two tours to choose from, the 'Road, River Splash Tour' which circles the castle and the Windsor Estate. The tour is split 50/50 between land and water. The 'River Splash Tour' goes straight to the river with more time spent on the water. Both tours last about 1 hour.

Ticket prices are around £18 for adults, £16 concessions, £12 Child (6-16), £6 Child (1-5), £1 Infant (under 1). Savings are available for family tickets.

It is advisable to book in advance either at **tickets@windsorducktours.co.uk** or on 01753 581158 or online at **www.windsorducktours.co.uk**

Getting There From London

Train – You can go from either London Waterloo to Windsor & Eton Riverside, taking 54 minutes, or London Paddington to Windsor & Eton Central (with a change at Slough) taking from 26 minutes to 35 minutes, depending on connecting trains. If you have a London Pass and have opted in to the Travel Package then this journey is included in your ticket, so no need to pay extra!

Car – About 30 miles from central London via the M4. Journey time should be around 50 minutes depending on traffic. There are no visitor car parks at Windsor Castle so you will need to use one of the Windsor town car parks, **www.windsor.gov.uk**

Coach – Various coach companies operate between London and Windsor. Try Green Line **www.firstgroup.com**, National Express or Megabus.

Tour Company – Premium Tours offer a morning trip to Windsor Castle which includes a morning tour of Windsor Castle followed by some free time to visit the town of Windsor. The tour starts at 8.15am and lasts for 5 hours. Adult tickets cost £55, Children £45, Concessions £52.

YORK

Once the Roman northern capital, York was founded in 71AD, and sits with the River Ouse flowing through it. The historic city is well known for its medieval buildings and of course the famous narrow cobblestoned street, The Shambles. York is a compact city and easily explored on foot.

What to do in York

The Shambles

VisitEngland/Diana Jarvis

Absolutely do not miss a walk down The Shambles. One of Britain's most famous streets. It is York's oldest street and Europe's best preserved Medieval street. The cobbled lane is lined with 15th century Tudor buildings, and is the most visited street in Europe.

The street was once lined with butcher's shops, but now is home to a variety of independent shops, cafes and restaurants.

This is one of the most unique streets I think I have ever walked down. The array of shops and quirky buildings are fascinating.

York Minster

VisitEngland/Diana Jarvis

The cathedral of York Minster is certainly a highlight when visiting York. The history of the site dates back to Roman times, with world famous stained glass windows on display.

Highlights include;

Undercroft Gallery – explore a series of interactive underground chambers, taking in 2000 years of history.

Climb the 275 steps up the central tower for fantastic views over the city (extra cost)

Listen to the choir sing – if you manage to catch a service you will be in for a treat as you listen to the choir sing. Check here for timings **www.yorkminster.org**

Free guided tour lasting about an hour, run by volunteers. The guides are incredibly knowledgeable and will happily answer your questions.

Admission – Adults £10 (£5 extra for the tower climb), Children are free with a paying adult (up to 4 children), Concessions £9 (£5 extra for the tower climb.) Children between 8 and 16 must pay £5 for the tower climb (under 8's not allowed.)

Opening – Monday to Saturday 9am until 5pm. Sundays 12.45 until 5pm. Please check the calendar for closures.

www.yorkminster.org – Deangate, Minster Yd, York YO1 7HH

Walk the City Walls

VisitEngland/Diana Jarvis

This is a great way to get a feel for the city and take in some fantastic views. The 13th century city walls are free to walk around and are a great, unique and alternative way to see the city. The walk should take between 1 and 2 hours, but you don't need to do all of it. If you don't have a lot of time, the best bit to see is the part with the views of the minster, from Monk Bar to Bootham Bar. Be careful with young children whilst on the walk.

Richard III & Henry VII Experience

Learn about the important influence of the two influential monarchs with the City Walls Experiences.

Richard III ruled England for 2 years from 1483 to 1485. He died at the age of 32 at the Battle of Bosworth Field during the War of the Roses. Richard III is an intriguing historical figure, being the last Plantagenet King to die. In 2012, the remains of Richard III were discovered by archaeologists. They were excavating an area beneath a car park in Leicester, in search of his final resting place.

Richard III was defeated at the Battle of Bosworth by Henry VII, and thus the start of the Tudor dynasty and Henry VII's reign began.

The Richard III experience showcases his life and the key battles of the Wars of the Roses. The experience takes place at Monk Bar, one of the four major fortified gateways to the city of York.

Henry VII ruled during the start of the Tudor period for a total of 24 years. The Henry VII experience offers interactive displays explaining life during Tudor times. The experience takes place at Micklegate Bar, another main gateway to the city. Micklegate Bar is the route where serving monarchs have entered York for almost 1,000 years. It is also where prisoners spent their last days and where the heads of traitors were put on display.

The Richard III experience is open 7 days a week from 10am until 5pm between April and October. From November until March it is open from 10am until 4pm.

The Henry VII experience is open 7 days a week from 10am until 4pm between April and October. From November until March it is open from 10am until 3pm.

Entry costs for 1 experience costs £3.50 for adults, £2 for children, £2.50 for concessions, and £9 for a family of 4 and £10 for a family of 5.

Entry costs for both experiences costs £5 for adults, £3 for children, £3.50 for concessions, £14 for a family of 4 and £14.50 for a family of 5. **www.richardiiiexperience.com**

The National Railway Museum
A fantastic place to spend a few hours, or longer if you really love trains. The biggest railway museum in the world, with a range of wonderful engines from days gone by, including steam and locomotive. See the Replica Rocket, a Japanese Bullet Train and of course the well-known Mallard. You can sit in parts of trains or just admire the variety of model trains on display. Entry is free and the museum is open every day from 10am until 6pm (closed 24th, 25th & 26th December.)

www.nrm.org.uk – Leeman Road, York, YO26 4XJ

York Castle Museum
An excellent museum, possibly one of the best in York. See the reconstructed Victorian street, wonder around it, taking in the sights, sounds and smells of York back in the Victorian age. Visit York Castle Prison and visit the cell of highwayman Dick Turpin! Other exhibitions include WW1, the exciting sixties and toys from the last 150 years.

Opening – Daily from 9.30am until 5pm. Closed on 25th, 26th December and 1st January. Closes at 2.30pm on Christmas Eve and New Year's Eve.

Admission – Adults (over 25) £10, Children under 16 are free, Access Ticket £5 (for visitors between the ages of 17 and 24 or on some income support, see website for full details.)

Address – York Castle Museum, Eye of York, York, YO1 9RY

Contact – **www.yorkcastlemuseum.org.uk** or 01904 687687 or email enquiries@ymt.org.uk

York's Chocolate Story
York is the UK home of chocolate. Learn all about the history of chocolate and even how to become a chocolatier on a York Chocolate Story Tour. York's Chocolate Story is set across 3 interactive zones, the Story Zone, the Factory Zone and the Indulgence Zone.

Opening – Open daily from 10am until 6pm (last tour at 5pm.) Closed 25th, 26th December and 1st January. Tours last about an hour and take place every 15 minutes.

Admission – £10.50 adults, £9.50 concessions, £8.50 children (4-15 years), Family of 4 £32.50, Family of 5 £39.50. Booking online in advance is recommended as tickets sell out quickly. Savings of up to 15% can also be made when booked in advance.

www.yorkschocolatestory.com – King's Square, York, YO1 7LD – 0845 498 9411

Tours within York

The Chocolate Trail

York is famous for its chocolate. Many big name chocolate bars (Kit Kat, Aero and Smarties to name a few) began life in York. Visit York offer a free Chocolate Trail which you can download from their website before you go or pick up in the tourist office in York. Learn how chocolate shaped York and find the chocolate themed cafes and shops around the city. What's not to like?

www.mediafiles.thedms.co.uk

Hop on Hop off City Sightseeing Tour

Starting in Exhibition Square and ending by Museum Gardens, with a duration of 1 hour. Hop on or off at any stop on the route. During the summer months buses run every 10 minutes. Adult tickets cost £12, Child £5, Concessions £8 and Family £28.

www.city-sightseeing.com

Free Walking Tour of York

Free walking tours leave from outside York Art Gallery in Exhibition Square. They last about 2 hours and end on The Shambles. Tour times are as follows;

1st November – 31st March, 10.15am and 1.15pm every day.

1st April – 31st October, 10.15am and 2.15pm every day.

1st June – 31st August, additional tours at 6.45pm.

There is no need to book in advance, just arrive at the departure point 5 minutes before the tour is due to start.

www.avgyork.co.uk

Eat and Drink

There is a huge selection of places to eat and drink in York, you will be spoilt for choice. There are so many pubs within the historic city, some say as many as 365, but as you only have 1 day here, that doesn't matter so much. As you would imagine, due to the age of York, many of the pubs have a rich history.

Ye Olde Starre Inn – One of York's oldest pubs dating back to 1644, serving classic British pub food, including pie and mash and hand battered fish and chips.

www.taylor-walker.co.uk – 40 Stonegate Walk, York, YO1 8AS – 01904 623 063

The Golden Fleece – Mentioned in the York Archives as far back as 1503. The Golden Fleece is one of England's most haunted sites and York's most haunted pub. Located opposite The Shambles, the Golden Fleece serves freshly prepared home cooked food between the hours of 11am and 8.30pm. Food and drinks are served in dining room, beer garden and bar areas.

www.thegoldenfleeceyork.co.uk – 16 Pavement, York, North Yorkshire, YO1 9UP – 01904 625171

Betty's Cafe Tea Rooms – Founded in 1919, the iconic tea rooms attract many visitors when in York. Serving delicious cakes and their famous afternoon tea. Open from 9am until 9pm serving breakfast, brunch, lunch and dinner.

www.bettys.co.uk – 6-8 St Helen's Square, York, YO1 8QP – 01904 659142

York Cocoa House – For chocolate lovers all over, head to York Cocoa House and indulge in a chocolate inspired lunch, or pop in for a hot chocolate and hand-made cake. York Cocoa House also run a chocolate school should you wish to try your hand at making something delicious.

www.yorkcocoahouse.co.uk – 3 Blake Street, York, YO1 8QJ – 01904 675787

Visitor Information Centre

1 Museum Street, York, YO1 7DT – **info@visityork.org** – Telephone – 01904 550099

Getting There From London

Train – The train goes from Kings Cross in London and takes less than 2 hours to get to York. Big savings can be made by booking far in advance (up to 12 weeks.) Book via **www.virgintrainseastcoast.com**

Car – Journey time without traffic is around 3 hrs. 40 minutes each way via A1 or M1. It is a long drive and for this reason I would really recommend the train.

THANK YOU

All that is left to say is a huge thank you for buying and reading this travel guide. Hopefully it is the first of many more guides to come. I really hope you enjoyed it.

Would you like to join my Readers List?

If you would like to join my readers list you can do so by signing up with your email address here.

www.uniquetravelguides.com/readers-list/

What happens on the readers list? Well, it is kind of like my newsletter where I will let you know when any future books or updated editions are released. They will always be either heavily discounted or free for readers on this list.

From time to time I might also let you know about anything else exciting going on in the world of **Unique Travel Guides**.

But, please know, I will never ever do anything else with your email address. No spamming, no annoying you, only good stuff, I promise! And if you want to leave the readers list, no problem. There is an easy unsubscribe button in each newsletter. You don't even need to tell me why!

Feedback

I would really love to know what you think of **33 Day Trips from London**. What did you like? What would you like more of?

You can let me know via 2 different ways. You can review this book on Amazon – that would be really great as it will help me become more visible to other potential readers. Alternatively you can contact me directly at **kate@uniquetravelguides.com** and let me know what you think. Or, you can do both! I don't mind.

I would also love to know what other travel guides you would be interested in. I have quite a few in mind, (probably too many for my poor fingers to type out!) but it would be great to know what you really want and need.

And that's all. I wish you all the luck in your travel planning and lots of fun and happy times on your travels. If you ever need any travel advice – you know where I am!

Happy travels,

Kate x

Made in the USA
Middletown, DE
30 June 2017